Stay Cheeky
G D Milne

Stay Cheeky Publishing

First Published in 2011 by

Stay Cheeky Publishing
Banchory
AB31 6LX

Copyright © 2011 G D Milne
All rights are reserved
No part may be produced in any form
without prior permission of the Publisher

ISBN: 978 0 9567810 0 0

Printed and bound in UK by
Antony Rowe Ltd.,
Chippenham, Wiltshire

Acknowledgements:

Deborah Leslie the author, www.deborahleslie.co.uk
for her continued support and for being a friend.

Alan Butchart, for his help with proofing.

My daughter Susan and grandson Allan, for their input.

My partner Alison, for assisting with everything and listening to my rants.

Rob Ward, for cover design.

The Lone Ranger & Tonto: First televised in the 50's. Dedicated to fighting the bad guys.

Skippy: First televised during the 60's. The bush kangaroo, always there to help in a crisis.

Stay Cheeky

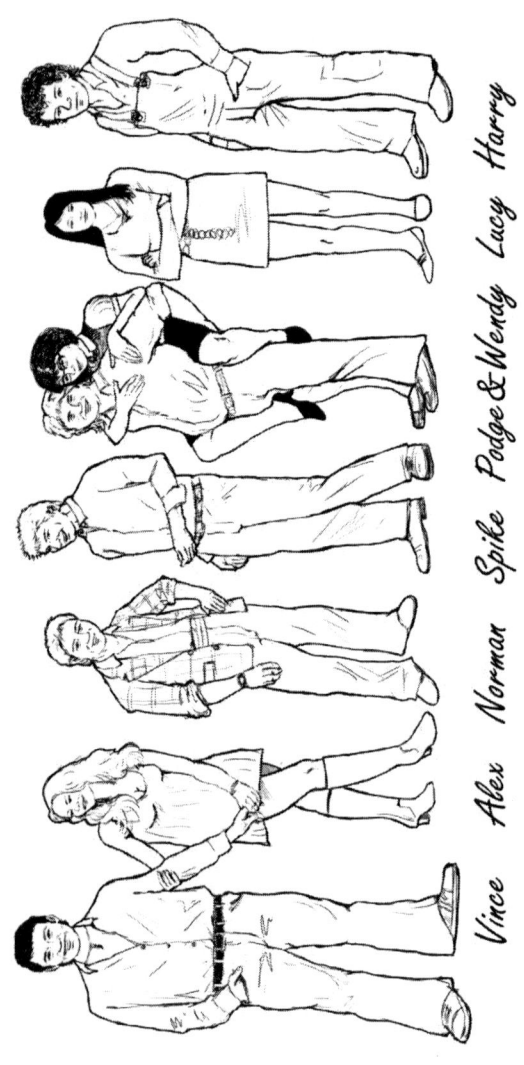

Chapter One
1965. Norman's Cake-Stand.

The holidays were over. It was time for new adventures, new routines and new teachers. The bus was full of shiny blazers and neatly pressed trousers, white socks and pleated skirts. They all looked different that day, more grown-up somehow. The boys' shoulders had broadened and the girls had blossomed. The bus was filling up as the vehicle made its way to the city academy. They were all aboard: Vince, Spike, Harry, Podger, Norman, Lucy and Wendy, soon to be split up to make their way to their different classes. Norman and Vince were in 1A, the others spread through 2B and C and 3A. Some were to have several teachers while most would have the same, albeit in different classes. The Rector would be there each morning at assembly. Mr Lattimer was a grey-faced man who glided around as if he were on castors, always with a clipboard held close to his chest.

'He looks dead,' Vince whispered in Norman's ear the first time that they saw him in the assembly hall.

'He probably is. He'll be wound up every day and pointed in this direction,' said Norman.

'Look for the key in his back,' Vince chuckled.

The routine was more or less the same for all the pupils. They would get a timetable with little boxes drawn on paper that was made up at the start of the week. There would be bells ringing at the end of the period. They would shuffle from one room to the next for English, Maths, History, Geography, Science and so on.

One of the classes which had to be attended once a week was Woodwork. The class had to work with saws, chisels and hammers. The teacher was Mr Munro, a likeable man, who would leave the pupils to get on with the job in hand. In this class there was none of the strict regime followed by most of the other teachers.

During one of his Woodwork lessons, Mr Munro quickly scribbled a drawing on the blackboard and instructed them to make a cake-stand. After telling the class to get on with it and also saying to take their time he went outside for a smoke. On his return, when he was making his inspection of the progress, he noticed Norman beavering away in the corner with a longer piece of wood than the rest of the class, totally engrossed in what he was doing.

'Norman! How are you getting on?' he shouted.

'Fine, OK, Mr Munro.'

'What are you making?' he called out.

'A coat-stand, like you said, sir.' Norman was now taking notice of what his fellow pupils were doing. They had stopped working and were creased with laughter.

'Howd'ya get the cakes up there?' shouted someone.

Norman, who had learned to live with his slight hearing disability, was quick off the mark. 'You throw them up, that's what you do.'

'Well, I think it's a fine-cake stand,' said Mr Munro. 'You carry on with what you are doing, the rest of you get a move on. You only have ten minutes left before the bell.'

The jibes were not finished with yet. Each pupil was allowed to take home their proud creation. On the bus that day, Norman's masterpiece had to stand in the passage and not in the overhead luggage compartment.

'Are you taking your Mum's chairs to school to get the legs made longer?'

'And, the table?' someone added.

'When's your Dad going to start work on the ceiling of your house?'

The laughter followed him all the way home to his bus stop. He wrestled with his creation down the passageway between the seats and out the door of the bus. The bus drove off with the rear window filled with laughing faces.

'Do you want a hand to carry it home?' asked Vince who came off at the same stop.

'No, I can manage fine,' Norman replied as he set off for his house with the piece of wood over his shoulder. He sat silently at the supper table that evening, having explained to his puzzled parents that the class had been making a cake-stand that day. Norman's cake-stand stood, pride of place, in the hallway for many years. It proved very handy for somewhere to hang your coat.

*

They filed in to room eleven for the English lesson, pushing and shoving as usual. At least this period wasn't as bad as Maths or History. The English teacher was Mrs Goddard, a woman in her early forties. She seemed a bit prim and proper and always wore pretty clothes, fashionable and expensive it seemed, not like some of the others. Most of the male teachers had tweed jackets with leather patches sewn on the elbows, or they wore old-fashioned suits, long overdue for the dustbin, grey or brown, rubbed shiny with all the years of wear and tear.

'Today we are going to read from Charles Dickens. Now I know that you have all heard of this famous man,' said Mrs Goddard.

'Yes,' someone muttered out of earshot. 'A helluva nice chap.'

The grubby books were handed round. This was often done by the teaching staff. They would hand out some books to get them reading and to keep the classroom quiet. It was sometimes done so that the teacher could catch up on some reading of her own, Woman's Weekly or some other magazine. With the slanted desk top, anything could be concealed from prying eyes. For all the class knew, the teacher could have been writing a recipe.

Take two eggs...half a pint of milk...some butter...

'Now, class, choose a chapter of your own choice to read. I expect you to write a short essay about what you have learned.'

'Oh good,' Vince thought. 'I'll pick the front cover. That looks pretty easy.'

Mrs Goddard settled behind her desk which was larger than the rest in the room. All that could be seen of her was her head and arms above the desk and her legs underneath.

Six ounces of flour...stir it in...

Vince had settled down with his book held just below

the eye line, positioning himself to look over the shoulder of the pupil in front of him. He had done this before. It gave him a direct line view of the teacher's legs. Mrs Goddard had the habit of crossing and uncrossing her legs, giving the class a good glimpse of her stocking tops. It was generally agreed that she did this on purpose for she often wore a wry grin of satisfaction.

Remember the salt and pepper...

'Vincent Wright,' she said the first time.

'Yes, Miss?'

'Get on with it,' she said with a scowl.

He checked to see if the book was the correct way up. She crossed her legs again.

'Vincent!' she said louder this time, her eyes staring wide at him as she crossed her legs again.

'Vincent!' she shouted.

The rest of the class were wondering what Odd Job could be doing. 'He wasn't scratching himself was he or picking his nose?'

The class settled down again in anticipation as to what would happen next. Vince was not the only pupil fascinated by the teacher's legs. The other boys were just as eager to look at Mrs Goddard's stocking tops but their position in the room did not offer the same view as the young Vincent Wright. Vince had chosen his desk right from the first day. It wasn't long before her voice was heard again.

'Vincent!'

'Yes, Miss?'

'Vincent, I want you to put down your book and stand up and tell the class what you have been reading about.'

'Well,' he started, clearing his throat. 'There was this fellow, Pip was his name and he eh...went to London to better himself and got a job eh... as a piper clearing out rats. He met this bloke eh...Fagin who sent him down chimneys...oh and eh...he had a cat as well and eh...a girlfriend called Stella and eh...she had just finished with a bloke called eh...Copperfield and...'

The class was amused. Mrs Goddard was not.

'Stop at once, Vincent! I have never heard so much rubbish in all my life. You will write a short essay all about Great Expectations and if you do not write it properly, I will have you sent to Mr Lattimer to be strapped. Do you understand?'

'Yes, Miss.'

'Now sit down.'

'Stupid bloody Dickens,' he muttered.

*

'Come on, who's going down town?' It was the lunch break and Vince was trying to get some people together for a jaunt to the city centre. The pupils would often go down town during the school mid-day break. They had a choice of going to the school canteen and exchanging their parents hard-earned money for a token to eat the food that was dished up, steaming and tasteless, or spend it on something more tasty like chocolate or crisps or in Podger's case, some buns from whatever tuck shop they passed along the route. It was not uncommon to see the academy pupils in blazers, blouses and pleated skirts mingling with the shoppers.

The number three bus was the quickest way for getting back and forth to the centre of town. It did mean that they had less money to spend on sweets but it was an acceptable trade off even if the fare had to be paid. The bus conductors were well aware of the fare dodgers that they had on board. It was an ongoing war between the bus company employees and the academy pupils. A favourite trick was for a boy or girl to get on at one of the stops before and try and stall the conductor upstairs, counting out change from his bag. A pound note, when available, was used by the children especially for that purpose. A number of them would be involved in the scam, getting a free ride on the bottom deck of the bus whilst the person who was upstairs was keeping the conductor busy for as long as they could. If the conductor came bounding downstairs before they had reached the stop at the town centre, then the school pupils would jump off from the open end at the back of the bus and walk the remaining distance. There was always someone nominated to delay the conductor by fumbling with coins or dropping them under the seat in front. The same system was used on the return journey after first checking where the conductor was on the bus. If he was spotted upstairs then the school gang would rush on the bus with one of them being nominated to go upstairs.

Chapter Two
1959. First Day at School.

Vince had arrived at the school gates of Berrydale Junior that historic day with trepidation, anticipation and constipation, the latter being a result of the diet that was normal for that time. Soon he would be introduced to the enema which was executed by Nurse Pringle with a skill acquired over many years.

'Hello, young man and what is your name?' asked this strange woman who was clutching a board with a list of names all neatly written in capitals.

'Vincent,' was the quiet reply.

'Ah, yes, Vincent. We are expecting you. Here you are,' she said, ticking another name off her list. 'My name is Miss Holby and I am your teacher. I'm sure you and I will get along just splendidly. Now come along and meet your class mates,' she continued, taking his hand to lead him into the building that was to be his introduction to the system.

Vince did not feel quite alone that day for he knew his pals were there. He also recognised some other faces, although their hair seemed to be combed out of recognition. Norman was there, along with Harry and

Lucy, friendly faces with which Vince had grown up. They had all been excited as the day approached, having discussed it in detail as they played in the fields and woods that was their domain. That first day at primary school went very quickly as they were all introduced to the regime of homework, books and pencils and playtime, a mixture of chatter and the opportunity to meet new friends. On the first day, at the break, Vince had been chatting to Spike and Robert who both lived close to the others in the village.

'Why are you called Spike? Miss Holby called you Ralph,' Vince asked.

'My Dad started calling me that as soon as I was born,' Spike replied. 'Dad helped when I was born. Mum couldn't get to hospital because of the snow so my Dad helped Nurse Pringle. Dad said that when I popped out I was pink and had a tuft of hair sticking up and he called me Spike. He always calls me that. My Mum gets annoyed when he does.'

The day had gone quickly and they were soon walking home to tell eager parents of their new adventure. Norman had stayed close to Vince that first day because Vince seemed to understand more than the rest of them about Norman's hearing difficulty. Norman was diagnosed with mastoid of the ear by the hospital after many visits and tests. It was to be a burden to him throughout his life.

'What did you think of today? Miss Holby is quite nice, isn't she?' enquired Vince of his chum.

'It was OK,' he replied, glad to get the first day over with. Although his parents had explained to the teacher about his condition, he had found it a strain to catch all of the day's proceedings and he would sleep a little uneasy that night. Vince had sensed the embarrassment that Norman had felt and somehow felt responsible for him. It was a friendship that was to last for many years. Spike, Robert and Harry along with Lucy and Wendy were to become part of the gang. They were all about to become firm friends and share many exploits together. Spike was born to be a troublemaker. He had a glint in his eye right from an early age. The others were an eager audience to his antics. By the end of that first day Spike seemed to be dirtier than the rest of them, his shirt tail hanging out, with one sock rolled up, the other at his ankles. Miss Holby had made him wash himself at the midday break but he still managed to look grimy as he made his way home. He had somehow managed to lose the skin from his knees during a playground scuffle. He would have the distraction of picking the scabs in the classroom some days later, much to the annoyance of Miss Holby.

Those early school years were a mixture of fun and laughter, playground fights and regular meetings behind the bicycle shed. It was here that Vince and his classmates were quickly learning the facts of life. Lucy had learned that by flashing her knickers she could hold the attention of all attending the bicycle shed meetings. Spurred on, she sometimes innocently pulled them down to her knees, causing much giggling and jostling for a closer look.

*

Vince's Mum had been the second generation of her family to settle in Berrydale, having been left the small cottage by her father. He had died quite a young man and Vince had only known his Grandad for a short time.

Vince seemed to remember that he was a quiet man who always had his pipe lit and hanging from his mouth. He had originally been from the Kerry region of Ireland and had settled in Berrydale, taking whatever work he could from the farming community after coming home from the war. The countryside in this part of Scotland with lush fields and rolling hills reminded him of home. He had been away in Europe at Hitler's war in the forties. Grandma O'Donnell had lived on in the cottage with her daughter Pamela, an only child. Pamela had met Matthew, Vince's father, at a dance in the city and after a brief courtship they had married and settled in the cottage with Pamela's Mum and Dad.

Vince came along ten months after the wedding and was four years old when Grandpa O'Donnell died. Matthew worked as a labourer with the local council. He had to depend on the bus service to get to town for a while. The bus company prided itself on always being on time. It would be a few years before Matthew could afford his own transport, an old, black Austin. Pamela had a part-time job at the post office helping out two afternoons a week. The pay was not good but every little helped, as Matthew's wage packet never seemed to go very far. The early years had them living on a meagre diet supplemented by whatever could be grown in the garden. Pamela would do her best to vary the daily intake of food but the fifties were not to be prosperous years. Only now and again was there some money for Grandma O'Donnell to enjoy the occasional glass of stout. She had acquired a taste for the brew on one of her visits to the Emerald Isle with Grandpa. Vince would never tire of the stories that his Grandma would tell of her spiritual home. They would be told over and over with a little variation here and there, much to the delight of the young Vincent Wright. Grandma O'Donnell told a grand story.

*

Apples were a luxury never to be bought, always to be acquired. The walk to school passed the widow McPherson's house and garden and in the garden stood a magnificent, old apple tree. Each year this tree was laden with fruit and to the eye of a small boy this was a challenge not to be ignored and had to be savoured. It was to be a food supplement for many years.

'Do you think they'll be sweet?' asked Spike, this particular day on the way home from school.

'No, they'll probably be sour,' replied Lucy.

'They'll be counted,' added Robert.

They knew from the seasons that had passed before that the apples were picked by the widow McPherson on the first week of October. Not one was allowed to fall to the ground it was said. Mrs McPherson made the finest chutney and a few jars were always on sale at the stall at the local hall on fête days. The gnarled, old tree was behind a large wall out of reach and even the branches would not extend over this obstacle except for one branch that maybe, just maybe, could be picked with a little ingenuity.

'If Lucy stood on Robert's shoulders, that branch there could be ours.' Vince pointed.

'She'll see us from the window,' piped up Norman.

'We'll come back when it's dark,' offered Robert.

'What about the dog?'

'The dog?'
'She doesn't have a dog.'
'She has.'
'When did she get a dog?'
'Must have been sometime last week.'
'It'll be a biting dog,' said Lucy.
'Not all dogs bite you,' Robert said.
'Patrick's one does and it farts a lot.'
'Yes, Harry was chased and got bitten on the leg.'
'Was it bad?'
'The nurse had a look at it and gave him a needle on his bum.'
'Did she stick that thing up his arse as well?'
'No, he had that last month.'

The group split up and went their separate ways, agreeing to meet up later after food and homework.

'By the way, does the widow McPherson have a dog?' asked Vince, bumping into Harry on the way to his house.

'Yes, Mum saw it when she went in past on Wednesday.'

'Is it a biting dog?'

'No, I think it's a Collie. Mum says she got it from somebody for nothing. The dog was too much bother and now Mrs McPherson has it. Patrick's dog bites. I was petting that thing when me and Dad were over looking for a tyre. It turned on me and nipped my leg and Mum called out the nurse. I had to have that needle on my backside. It's very sore. You'll know when you stroke that beast and it starts to fart, you'd better run. It farts when you stroke it.'

'It farts all the time. Do you think that if you went to

buy a dog at the kennels at Burnside you could choose? Can I have a farting dog please?'

'I know,' Harry giggled. 'What about the smell? What if the minister came in past?'

'Listen, we're going to get some of the widow McPherson's apples tonight. If you can get away we'll be in the lane just as it gets dark.'

'OK, I'll try.'

Later that evening the apple raiders were assembled just as darkness fell. Robert was the last to arrive, puffing his way up the lane due to the weight that he had already amassed. He was destined to be a heavy kind of lad right through puberty and well into his teens. The gang, led by Vince, crept along the wall in single file.

'Shut up you lot,' he whispered, 'she'll hear us.'

They arrived at the chosen spot where the branch, laden with apples was sticking out.

'Right,' Vince whispered to the others. 'Robert, you're the heaviest and Lucy is the lightest. Lucy, you get up on Robert's shoulders. We'll hold you. See if you can stand up and reach that branch.'

Robert bent down and stuck his head through Lucy's legs. He had been eager and excited about being chosen as anchorman as she still had her school uniform on. Up she wobbled, supported by Vince and Spike with Robert holding her legs as high up as he dared.

'Can you reach it?' Robert was tempted to say *yes*, but thought better of it.

'Lucy, can you reach it?' repeated Vince.

'Robert, is that as tall as you can stand?' Lucy whispered from above.

'Yes,' said the voice from somewhere beneath the pleats of her skirt.

'It's no good. I can't reach. I'm coming down,' she said, turning herself round to slide on to Robert's shoulders.

'Robert, let me down quickly!' she snapped. He was still out of sight, somewhere between her thighs.

'I'll have to do it myself,' said Vince. 'C'mon, give us a hand up.' Quick as a flash, he was up on Robert's shoulders. He could just brush the apples with his fingers. By standing up on tiptoe he could reach the branch and get his balance right. By this time Robert's shoulders were starting to get sore and anyway it was less fun looking up Vincent's bum.

'Hurry up, I'm getting tired,' was just uttered, when the dog came thundering down the garden, barking ferociously. It threw itself at the wall and all that Robert saw in that instant was the mouth and teeth inches from his face. 'Oh shit,' he gasped as he fell backwards and onto the path. Quickly gathering himself up, he and the others were off at a very quick pace, leaving Vince hanging from the branch, flying over the wrong side of the wall. The dog had managed to jump up and attach its teeth to his trouser leg.

'Who's there?' shouted a female voice from the house door. 'What's going on?' The widow McPherson could just make out the outline of her dog swinging back and forth with what appeared to be a very acrobatic young person. 'You leave my apples alone, you little hooligan!' she cried, brandishing a sweeping brush. 'I'll heat your backside for you!'

The branch on the tree could no longer support this double act and with a resounding crack Vince found himself falling on to the wall. Temporarily winded, he had to gather himself together. The dog was still attached to his leg and with the added leverage of four paws was trying to drag him back to the other side of the garden wall. With a quick flick of his leg, Vince managed to shake the dog off, resulting in the two of them parting company with Vince landing on his head still clutching some apples. The widow McPherson and her dog were taking it in turns shouting and barking. Vince picked himself up and limped away, noticing the distinct lack of support from his chums. He eventually found them far away from the drama.

'Where have you been? I could have used a bit of help. Thanks very much.'

'We're not arguing with that mutt. It bites.'

'Yes, I noticed. I had it swinging on my leg. I could have been eaten alive.'

'Well, how many did you get?' asked Robert.

'These three. No thanks to you, you little podger, and the rest of you.'

'Is that all?'

'Well, you all go back then. See if you can do better,' snapped Vince as be bit into one of the apples.

'Let's have a taste then, we've been waiting here for ages,' said Lucy as the apples were handed round.

'Mmm, they're so sweet,' dribbled Robert, taking a larger bite than the others. 'We'll have to get a lot more next time.'

The rest of them nodded in agreement. They were not

too disappointed with their evening's work.

'Right, where is he?' asked Nurse Pringle. She had been summoned by Mrs Wright. The castor oil had not worked in spite of the twice daily dosage.

'He's around here somewhere, Nurse. Vincent, where are you? The nurse is here.'

He had not been looking forward to this moment. The castor oil had been bad enough but now he had to have that thing up his bum. Spike had already had it done and went into great detail at school one day, much to the amusement of all, including Vince. He knew there was no alternative. He would be glad to clear his back passage as it was distinctly uncomfortable. He had not been on the pot for three days. He crept out of his room to where the nurse stood, observing briefly the large syringe and bowl lying on the table.

'Right, lad, down with your trousers and bend over this chair.' Nurse Pringle was a tall, heavy-set woman with hair tied up in a net. She was rarely seen without the uniform that she wore.

'Stop shaking, lad! After this you'll be able to sit down properly.' And with that reassuring remark, she stuck the syringe up Vince's back passage.

'Oohh!' he groaned, hoping his outburst might attract a gentler approach. He felt the liquid enter his body. The nurse was now holding the bowl to his bum but nothing was happening.

'Relax lad, and let it go.'

'Oh! Oh!'

'OK, let's have another go,' said the nurse, slapping him. She was about to enter again when a great sensation went through Vince's body. The sigh of relief could just be heard by the two women present. Quick as a flash the nurse had the bowl in her hand once more, just in time to catch what was coming out of Vince's rear end. For Vince, this was now a very pleasant sensation. He cried with the relief it gave him.

'Goodness me lad, I'll bet your glad to get rid of that. That's the oddest jobby I've seen for a while. Now pull up your trousers,' she said, giving his bum a wipe. 'You eat more roughage from now on, or I'll be back.'

Vince nodded, still with an expression of relief on his face. He made a mental note that he was going to listen to the nurse from now on and eat more roughage, whatever that was.

'You make sure that he gets more cabbage and turnips and pour the castor oil into him regular. That will keep him in good condition.'

'Thank you, Nurse,' Pamela said, glad that her little boy was back to normal.

At school the next day Vince found himself comparing notes with Spike.

'I had to have the nurse last night, same as you had.'

'Did she stick that thing up your arse?'

'Yes.'

'Did it work?'

'Yup, she said it was an odd jobby that I did.'

'Why?'

'Don't know. I was glad to get rid of it.'

'Well, you'll be able to sit down again, won't you? Have you told Harry?'

'No, I suppose he'll hear about it and tell the whole

school.'

'Well if he doesn't, I will,' said Spike, running off laughing.

'Bugger, I wish I hadn't told him now. It'll be all over the school, they'll be laughing at me for days,' thought Vince.

'Come and see this!' It was Spike, shouting from the corner of the bicycle shed.

'Hoi, Vince, odd jobby. Hoi Odd Job! Come here, c'mon, come over here, you're missing this. Lucy has a different colour of knickers on.'

Vince ambled over as casually as he could to join the others at the bike shed.

'Hoi, Odd Job, come and have a look at this.'

Lucy had changed her underwear from navy to white. There was something more exciting about the show today.

*

Patrick was a strange soul with a slight foreign accent that did not offer a clue as to his place of origin. He had moved to the area before the youngsters had been born. He kept to himself and seemed to make a living as blacksmith and scrap dealer. He was neither liked nor disliked but he was filthy. The dirt and grease that hung from him always made him dirty. He also had a habit of picking his nose and rolling it on his dirty overalls. Pick a bit, roll, change hands, pick, swap over fingers, roll and when he had accumulated enough he would pop it into his mouth much to the disgust of anyone observing. He also had a dog that had no name and farted a lot. He hadn't seen the point of giving the animal a title when shouting and yelling at the poor thing would be just as effective to get its attention. If it was in his way, a swift kick up the arse got the message across. So that was Patrick: filthy, grumpy, recycling bogies as well as scrap. Then there was his dog: filthy, grumpy, sore arse and a farting habit.

*

'Come on in you lot, the water's lovely.' They had walked up to Patrick's pond. None of them could swim. They thought they could. They had watched the ducks. 'Easy, you just thrash your legs about, don't you?'

'Bloody hell, Spike. It's freezing!'

'Come on, you bunch of softies.'

They were standing stripped to their underwear but wanted a better reason to go in the water than was being demonstrated. Patrick was away for the day. His dog was locked up. They could hear it barking in the distance.

Lucy shoved Vince in the water and Norman and Harry were soon to follow with a loud splash. Podger was still on the bank, clutching the remains of a sandwich that he had left the house with.

'Hurry up, Podge.'

'That's how you catch cold,' he said, shivering.

'Let's build a raft, look at all the wood and stuff floating around.'

There was a lot of trash in the pond, proving quite an obstacle course for the ducks, particularly if the wind was blowing the wrong way.

'You need oil drums first!' shouted Podger, his mouth full of bread and butter. 'There's two over there,' he continued, pointing to the pile of Patrick's mess.

'Well, go and get them and we'll get started.'

Podger popped the last of the sandwich in his mouth

and set off to get the oil drums that were floating further down the pond. He picked them up one at a time and hurled them over towards the others. They quickly had an old green door lashed down on the drums with some rope that they had found. They were taking it in turns to jump on board for it could only support two or maybe three at a time.

'It's my turn now, get off. We need to have a go.' They were starting to squabble. This was proving to be great fun. 'Why hadn't they built a raft before now?' they thought.

'I'm the captain, *Captain Lucy*.'

'Get off, I want a go.'

Podger had found a couple of planks that would improvise as oars. He was in the water by now, supervising proceedings. Lucy and Spike were on the bridge with Vince hanging on to the sides. Podger had somehow managed to hoist himself onto the platform and now there were four of them balancing on the raft.

'I name this ship *The Jolly Podger*.' They fell about laughing.

'Podge, stand still for Christ's sake!' They were well out in the deepest part of the pond by now.

'Podge, sit down. You're making it unsafe.' The raft was rocking from side to side, gathering momentum.

'Everyone sit down!'

Spike was the first to go. He fell into the water, causing the raft to be even more unstable.

'Man overboard!' The ropes binding the platform to the drums snapped with a loud twang. 'Oh, bugger!' someone shouted. Vince, who had been rowing with the makeshift oars, landed on his back with the planks of wood flying through the air. One of them landed on Spike's head just as he had managed to grab the side. Down he went again, gasping for air. The ducks had stopped feeding by now. They were all lined up as if watching the proceedings. The raft had broken up with everyone in the water. Podger grabbed Lucy. The two of them were both bobbing in the water like corks. Everyone was accounted for except Spike who was having a bad time underwater. Had it not been for a quick-thinking Vince, the outcome might have been more serious. He dived down and grabbed Spike by the pants and they kicked their way to the surface, both gasping for air.

'That water tastes horrible!' spat Spike, looking like a drowned rat.

'Well, stop spitting it on me,' replied Vince.

'Get your hands off my drawers, I can manage now.'

Somehow they all scrambled to the bank. The only evidence that was left was two oil drums floating in the breeze and the odd piece of wood. They could hear Patrick's dog barking in the distance and the sound of a vehicle approaching up the dirt road.

'Bugger, it's Patrick, let's get out of here.'

They started running down the road, some half-dressed, some still in their underwear, clutching their clothing to the sounds of, 'Gettafuck you shites! Bugger off, shites!'

Podger had been off first. He always needed a head start. The others caught up quickly just as he stumbled and fell, setting off a chain reaction. They piled into him, scattering like ninepins. The heap of bodies lay on the grass verge, laughing their heads off.

'It's OK, we're safe. The grumpy old bugger's gone.'

They dried themselves as best as they could, rubbing their hair with the clothes that they had.

'C'mon, let's get dressed. I wonder what's for supper. I'm starving.'

'Me too,' said Podger.

Chapter Three
1962. A Wheel for the Bike.

All the boys had bicycles of some sort except Vince. He had the makings of one. The old Raleigh from Matthew's younger days had been hanging in the shed but it had a buckled front wheel and the chain needed fixing. The tube on the good wheel would need a patch which would be easily sorted out. It was a task that Vince was determined to tackle that Tuesday after school.

'What are you doing tonight?' Vince asked Norman during the midday break.

'Dunno, Mum said she wants a hand with the garden. Why?'

'I want to go to Patrick's yard to get a wheel for my bike.'

'Are you going to steal it?'

'If he's there I'll have to offer him something for it. I'll come past your house anyway.'

'OK.'

That afternoon went pretty quickly. They made heads of papier-mâché for the puppet show in the classroom. They tore up the paper, soaked it and shaped it round the cardboard tube from a toilet roll. It was proving great fun and they had to get the shape right. It would be set hard by the morning.

The children made their way home that day, the boys' white, spindly knees showing below their short trousers. The noise from their heavy, tacked boots stopped clattering only when they paused to see if they could catch the rabbit in the roadside ditch, but it was too fast for them.

'Mum, I'm home, what's for supper?'

'Cabbage stew.'

'Oh, no,' he thought, 'cabbage stew, again.'

'Have you any work to do for school?' Pamela asked.

'No, I'm fixing the bike tonight. I want to see if Patrick has a wheel for it. Can you give me some money?'

'I gave you my change yesterday. What've you spent it on?'

He hadn't spent it at all. It was always worth a try.

'Change your clothes before you go out. You only have one good pair of trousers, you know. I'm not having them ruined. Put on your old pair.'

The cabbage stew was quickly eaten along with a plate of pudding that followed. Vince left the table and was off round to Norman's place.

'Hello Mrs Halford, is Norman here?' He had gone round the back to the garden, having had no response from the front door.

'He's over there in the corner, helping me with the weeds.'

'Can he come out?'

'What are you two up to?'

'Nothing much, I'm going up to Patrick's for a wheel

for my bike.'

'Is it OK, Mum?' Norman had had enough of gardening for the time being.

'Go on then. Don't be back late and make sure you get washed before bedtime.'

'Thanks, Mum.'

'Have you got any money?' asked Norman.

'I got some from Mum yesterday.'

The two of them went off to find a wheel, moving to the verge to let old Brodie past in his tractor and cart. His place was further up the hill. He had to use part of the road to the scrap yard before he swung off and over the grid that kept his sheep in.

Brodie was a cheery man with a rosy complexion and a permanent smile. He and his wife farmed a smallholding, raising sheep and cattle, a milking cow, a scattering of hens, the odd cat and a sheepdog. He liked children. Vince and his friends were always made welcome even when they were helping themselves to the brambles that grew in abundance around the edges of Brodie's fields. At hay time the children always made a point of visiting the farm to watch and sometimes assist, as Brodie pulled the small stacks of hay with his tractor. They would help him with the chain that went round the bottom and jump on the stack as he pulled away. Brodie's dog would be there with its tail wagging, eager to see if this stack had a mouse nest under it. The children had great fun chasing the mice but never seemed to catch as many as the dog. He reigned supreme in the fields. He was a far better micedog than he was a sheepdog.

They arrived at Patrick's to see the scrap man in his

smithy with the fire going full blast. He was hammering out a piece of metal on the anvil. The dog noticed them first and trotted over, causing them to stop in their tracks.

'It's OK, Norman. It won't bite. It's just being nosey.'

'Are you sure?'

'Hello doggie.'

The dog looked at them, had a sniff, farted and went back to where it had been sleeping. Patrick had stuck the metal bar back in the furnace and was enquiring, 'Whad ye want?'

'We need a bike wheel. Have you got one?'

'Over there. Have a look yourself,' he growled and turned back to the red-hot metal bar.

After a lot of rummaging, they found a wheel that looked right. Vince held it by the baffle while Norman spun it to check it was not buckled.

'This'll do us.'

'How much money have you got?' asked Patrick.

'I've only got sixpence.'

'Well, give us that then.'

On the way home they had just reached the lane at the end of the road when they noticed the van parked in the small area that was partially hidden by the steep sided bank. They had to have a look. This was a favourite spot for couples in the evening, stopping to have a smooch. They crept up the blind side and peered over the top of the bank.

'Can you see?' whispered Norman.

'Yes, look, the fellow has his hands on her boobs. She's got her blouse off.'

'Is he trying to get milk out of there?'

'Naw, that only happens after they've had babies.'
'What?'
'It only happens when they've had babies,' said Vince, raising his voice.
'Who's there?' The man, hearing the noise, was half-way out of the van door. The woman was quickly grabbing her blouse. He briefly saw the faces of the two lads peering at him from the gloom.
'I'll kick your arses!' he shouted. That would not have been possible. The two rogues were well away by this time, pausing briefly to pick up the bike wheel. They ran the rest of the way home, chuckling to themselves. They opened the garage door and hoisted the bicycle down from the hook, banging Norman on the head.

'Bugger, that's sore!'
'Sorry, Norman.' Vince was in a hurry to get his bike working.
'Where's the spanner?'
'Over there in Dad's tool box. Remind me to put it back. I'm going to get a basin of water for the tube. You take off the front wheel, will you?'

Pamela had just finished washing up the dishes in the sink.

'Did you get what you wanted, Vincent?'
'Yes, Mum, me and Norman are fixing it now. Can I have a basin of water?'
'You make sure you finish what you're doing tonight. I want you to help me with the garden tomorrow.'
'It's OK. This won't take long. I need two spoons as well, for the tyre.'
'Help yourself but I don't want them back bent out of

shape.'

Vince was back in the shed with the tools needed for the job.

'We'd better hurry up, Norman. Mum's got me gardening tomorrow after school.'

Norman and Vince soon had the wheel in place and the other one patched and blown up. The chain proved more difficult. They found the link they were looking for. It still needed brake blocks on the rear but that would have to wait. Before it got dark they set off down the road with Norman on the handlebars, his chum pedalling.

*

'Vincent, is that you?'

'Yes, Mum.'

'How was school today?'

'Oh, just the usual, the toilets are still frozen. We had to go to the wood again.'

This was the second day of extremely cold weather, the school lavatories were not working and Miss Holby had instructed all the children to assemble in the playground. 'Right, to the woods!' she commanded and they all set off the short distance to the wooded area behind the school. It had been something of an adventure the day before. They had gone single file led by the teacher. Some of them had been given the responsibility of carrying the toilet paper, to be passed around when required. They arrived at the temporary toilets. The girls were separated from the boys, much to their disappointment.

'Right, children, find a tree and do your business and no nonsense,' she said, casting an eye over the regular trouble makers.

'What'd she say?' Norman asked the person nearest to him.

'She said that you've to go over there.' Spike pointed to where he had seen Lucy disappear. 'Behind that clump of bushes.'

Norman set off as told and was just starting to relieve himself amidst a juniper bush when a scream was heard from the other side. It was Lucy who had been crouching down doing her business when a jet of urine had landed on the back of her head.

'What's going on?' was the cry from the teacher.

'Someone's peeing on me, Miss.'

'Norman, what are you doing there? Come out at once. You should be over with the other boys.'

'What?'

'Come out of there at once!'

'Sorry, Miss, I was told to go over here.'

'Who told you? It was Ralph or Vincent wasn't it?'

Norman, having just remembered who had given him the instructions, was having a problem holding back his amusement at the situation.

'It is not funny, you dirty boy, look at poor Lucy's hair. I will deal with you when we get back to the class room. All of you hurry up!' she snapped, addressing the plume of steam that was rising from the wood.

The rest of the day was different for Norman. He had to sit by himself in the cupboard usually reserved for the cleaning materials.

'Vincent, listen to me, we need someone to deliver the telegrams. Mr Jeffries is getting old and he isn't as fit anymore. I've told him that you will do it.'

'Aw, Mum,'

'Don't *Aw Mum* me.' The post office pays half a crown for each delivery and it's only now and again that we get telegrams anyway.'

'OK,' he replied, thinking that half a crown was a pretty good deal for a short trip on the bike.

'Alright, you can deliver them after school or at weekends should any come in. If there are any that have to go out first thing, I'll go with them myself.'

That same week Vince was called upon to deliver a telegram to a house over in the valley. It was just as well he had spent some time fixing his bicycle, tightening and oiling the chain. It was a pity that he had not given more attention to the brakes. On the return journey he had been going too fast and not been able to control his machine when rounding a corner. He hit a dry-stone wall full force and it was at that moment he became an astronaut, resulting in a badly bruised shoulder and a ruined jacket. It also meant he would have to pay a visit to Patrick's yard in search of another wheel. He would have to be more careful in future. This job was proving to have too many overheads.

Chapter Four
1963. Ferguson's Caravan.

'What's he doing with that?'

'What?' Vince turned to see Ferguson, pulling a shiny white caravan behind his Land Rover. He was slowly making his way up the road, turning into the grassy area at the rear of his house.

'We better go and see,' said an inquisitive Harry, picking up his bike and setting off with urgency. 'C'mon, Odd Job, hurry up!' He pedalled off to get a better look with Vince running behind, cursing the fact that he had not fixed his bike after his collision with the dry-stone wall. Vince caught up with Harry who had now found a tree that offered a better view. The two of them perched themselves on a stout branch.

'Why is he putting it in the field and not beside the house?'

'Dunno, probably needs to get the tractor past.'

'He'll be going his holidays in it.'

'He never goes on holiday. He'd have to spend money if he did.'

'We'll have a look when he's at the Mart on Friday. Has it got curtains?'

'It's hard to see from here,' was Harry's reply, his

voice trailing off as he slipped from the branch.

'Bugger!'

'Are you OK?'

'No, I've landed in some kind of poo and it's on my trousers.'

'Hang on a second, let's have a look.' Vince climbed down for a closer inspection.

'Yuk! That's fresh stuff, how did you manage to aim for that?'

'Can you scrape it off?'

'No chance, do it yourself. Use this stick... Here.'

'Go on, give us a hand.'

'No, it's bloody honking.'

'I can't reach it.'

'Then roll on the grass.'

Harry managed to get the worst of the cowpat removed with the aid of a tuft of grass he had pulled. They set off for home, Vince in front upwind, chuckling to himself, Harry following, cursing Ferguson's herd of cows.

'You're not coming in the house with those trousers!' shouted Harry's Mum, Dorothy, with his younger sister Rosemary. Dorothy had captured the aroma just as Harry was walking up the front steps.

'Look at the state of your trousers. Get them off this minute. Why do you always have to come home in a mess? What are you laughing at Vincent Wright? Is this your doing?'

'No, Mrs Roberts. It was an accident.'

'Stinky poo, stinky poo,' said Harry's little sister.

'And, what about the smell that you always make, Runny Nose?'

'My name is Rose!' said the little girl, stamping her feet.

'Yes, it's short for Runny Nose.' Harry liked calling his sister that name to annoy her.

'Mummy, Mummy,' she started to cry.

'It's alright, my little pet. Harry didn't mean it.'

'Yes I did,' he continued, moving to one side to avoid the kick that his sister aimed at him.

Harry's parents had not planned for a second child. Rosemary had arrived three years previously and was a cherished part of the family or at least she was to her parents. From Harry's perspective, she was a little brat. The two of them were always fighting. Rosemary wanted to be with her older brother and his friends, and Harry's Mum encouraged him to take his sister along to some of the meeting up with friends, much to Harry's annoyance. The rest of the youngsters didn't seem to mind the presence of this little girl. She didn't get in the way of their grown-up discussions. She would much rather play with her imaginary friend *Purp*. This was some kind of purple urchin to whom Rose would talk endlessly, particularly before she went to sleep at night. Where this figment of her imagination came from was a mystery to all including Rose's Mum. On the occasions when Harry was roped in to taking his sister along with him, the two of them could be seen walking along the village with Harry well out in front and Rose trying to catch up. She would be in conversation with her invisible friend, chattering away in a world of her own.

'You're a stinky poo,' she said, having another attempt at a sneaky kick.

'Stop it, Runny Nose. Mum, she's trying to kick me again.'

Harry had his sister by the hair. He was still managing to avoid her attempts to maim him.

'That's enough, young man. Stop being bad to your sister.' Harry was too slow to avoid his mother's hand as it made contact with the back of his head.

'Ouch, Mum!'

Vince was chuckling to himself. He was enjoying this.

'Stinky Poo, Stinky Poo.'

'Runny Nose, Runny Nose.'

'Will you two stop? I'll get your father to deal with you when he comes back. Now go inside and get changed, Harry.'

'She started it. Why don't you go and speak to your purple friend, Runny Nose, or has he got fed up with you as well?'

'Mummy, he's being bad to me and Purp.' This time she managed to catch him on the ankle.

'Ouch!' Harry made a grab for the little brat but was stopped by his mother.

'Get inside now, both of you. Say goodbye to Vincent.'

'See you later, Odd Job.'

'Yeah, bye Harry, bye Run...eh...Rose.'

Vince, who was glad that his parents had not landed the burden of a sister on him, was still grinning when he found his Mum in the kitchen preparing the supper.

'What have you been up to, Vincent?'

'Nothing much, Mum. I was with Harry. He landed in some cow shite.'

'What did you say?'

'I was with Harry. He fell in some cow manure. He doesn't half smell. Mum, why don't I have a sister?'

'Why? Do you want one? Would you like a little sister for company?'

Vince hadn't quite grasped how babies were made. He knew that they came from the body somewhere. For a while he thought that they came out of the back passage but he dismissed that theory after a big discussion in the school playground. Someone had pointed out that if the babies arrived this way, how do you stop them going down the toilet. Norman's offering was even worse. He was convinced that you just collected them from hospital when you had saved enough money. Spike was the wisest it seemed. He had a little more information than the rest of them, having been told by his parents about his own delivery aided by Nurse Pringle. It was agreed that they came out the front bit but they would have to be terribly small. Podger's contribution was based around eggs but he felt that he should learn more about the subject if he was to maintain his status in the group. They approached Lucy to comment on the matter and confirm their suspicions but she wasn't that much help to them, although she did introduce a new word called the womb. Norman had been straining to hear and had to ask Spike what the wood had to do with it. They would have to pursue this matter further just to clear things up. They were even more confused when they attended Lucy's cabaret act behind the bicycle shed. They had thought that a closer inspection would solve the mystery, but to no avail. It took Podger's determination to clear matters up.

He had plucked up the courage to ask his Dad one night much to his parent's surprise. Mr Chalmers had done his best to explain the facts of life to his offspring and was very pleased with his rendition, glad that he had got that over with. The word quickly spread around the school, finally dispelling all that stuff about fairies and bushes.

'Well, Vincent. You haven't answered my question. Would you like a little sister?'

'Naw, Mum. Can I have a football instead?'

*

Berrydale was a quiet hamlet sitting in the heart of Scotland amidst magnificent hills and rolling fields. It was mostly a farming community with a population of one hundred and fifty seven living in houses scattered over a large area. Berrydale had a church and graveyard, post office, community hall, general store, a pub and a bus service that had buses that were generally always on time. Vince and his friends lived very close to one another and the parents were always in touch even if it was a quick hello whilst passing. Most houses had a garden where a mixed variety of vegetables would be grown to supplement the diet.

*

She arrived on the Friday evening by car with her mother and father and a white terrier dog. This arrival would have gone unnoticed had Vince not been taking a shortcut back to the house. He bumped into her as she was exploring the wood by the lane leading to Patrick's pond.

'Hello,' she said.

'Hello,' he stuttered.

'Do you live here?' she asked.

'No...I mean yes...I mean I'm over there.' Vince pointed to the row of houses visible through the trees. Just at that moment the dog came thundering round the corner, crashed into his leg and started jumping on him.

'Sebastian! Stop that, get down.'

'Does it bite?'

'No, he's being friendly,' she replied.

'What's your name?' she asked.

'Vincent, Vince, but I'm called Odd Job.'

'Why are you called that?'

'Because I deliver telegrams sometimes,' he lied. 'Are you lost?'

'I'm on holiday with my Mum and Dad. We're staying with Mr Ferguson for two weeks. My name's Julie and I'm from Ardrossan in Ayrshire,' she said all in one breath and in a funny voice.

'Where's that?' he asked.

'It's beside Glasgow,' she replied.

It was then that he noticed the bumps on her front and he thought she must be twenty years old. 'Have you got a job?'

'No, silly, I'm at school in Ardrossan.'

'Funny,' he thought, 'Lucy and Wendy haven't got bits like that.'

'Anyway, I have to go. Will I see you later?'

'Yes, I hope so. Are your holidays the same as we have?' he asked, noticing that she had big teeth as well.

'We go back on the third,' was her answer. 'I have to go. My Mum will be looking for me. Bye. Come on, Sebastian,' she shouted in that funny voice she had.

'Woof, woof!' Sebastian seemed to have a normal

voice.

'Hello,' it was Harry, pedalling furiously to catch up just as Vince reached the gate.

'What have you been doing? Have you seen Norman?'

'No, I've been with Julie.'

'Who's Julie?'

'She's from Ardrossan in Ayrshire.'

'Where's that?'

'It's beside Glasgow. She's on holiday. She's staying at Ferguson's with her Mum and Dad and dog Sebastian.'

'Is it a farting dog?'

'Probably.'

'Is she pretty?'

'Yes, she has big teeth and big lumps.'

'What, on her face?'

'No, stupid. Her boobs are huge.'

'You saw them?'

'They stick out. They're huge.'

'Does she have a bra?'

'I don't know. We can get her to go swimming with us in the pond. Don't tell Spike. I saw her first.'

The two weeks passed quickly with Vince fascinated by his new found friend, half girl, half woman. One hot day, they persuaded Julie to go to the pond and the boys were delighted when she got very wet along with the rest of them. Spike had been trying his best to impress the girl from Ardrossan but she seemed to favour Vince. They had been enjoying sneaky kisses and cuddles at every opportunity. She would always be Vince's first love. Julie and her dog were to return the following year to rekindle their friendship and enjoy more stolen kisses and language lessons. Vince liked the way she talked, calling children *weans*. She had been home with Vince to his house for tea and biscuits. Pamela liked this mature, young lady who had bewitched her little boy. The two lovebirds had enjoyed days together, taking turns on Vince's bike. She would sit on the handlebars with her hair blowing in his face. Sometimes he couldn't see to navigate and they would fall in a heap with Sebastian leaping on top of them, not wanting to be left out of the fun. They would hold hands like grown-ups and speak about when they'd be married and live in a big house with lots of weans and cats and dogs and go on long walks. It was sad that first year when they had to say goodbye. That day they had exchanged love letters just before Julie drove off with her parents back to Ardrossan in Ayrshire.

'She'll be back again,' said Pamela, giving her little boy a hug.

'I'm not worried,' replied a gloomy Vince. He was miserable for the next few days. Not even the thought of Lucy's cabaret act at school could cheer him up.

*

'Let's go up to Brodie's,' said Harry. It was a fine September's day. The sun was shining. School was over for the weekend and they were bored. Wendy, Norman and Vince had met up with Harry. The rest of the gang would catch up with them if they wanted to. They knew that Lucy was going into town with her Mum to do some shopping. Spike was around somewhere and Podger was probably still at breakfast.

'Are we taking the bikes?' asked Norman.

'Nah, let's leave them. I'm walking,' said Vince. 'You

lot please yourselves.'

Wendy didn't have a bike so she was always at the rear on the rare occasions that she joined the rest of them. They liked having her along. She didn't mind being teased about being the minister's daughter. Wendy was quite small for her age. She was a little plump with a friendly, smiley face. She had dark, wavy hair and was quietly spoken. Her father, the Reverend Calder, was a familiar figure at the church service on a Sunday. He also did the services for most of the weddings and funerals and looked in past all in the village from time to time, with particular attention to the elderly and sick. He was known to like an occasional drink. The bottle nearly always came out of the sideboard when he made a visit. *The Reverend Calder: Available for births, deaths, marriages and the occasional libation.*

'Wonder what Patrick's up to?' asked Harry as they made their way up past the pond. They could hear him in the distance, grinding some metal.

'He'll be cutting up some cars or something.'

'Look, there's an old pram. I'm going to have a look.' Wendy was off and over to the pile of junk that was scattered around the pond.

'Give us a hand somebody.'

They pulled off the rubbish on top to reveal the pram which had probably been discarded by someone whose offspring had outgrown it.

'It's in good nick. The wheels are good as well. C'mon, get it out and on the road. We'll see how it runs.'

The pram was inspected in great detail. It had four sturdy wheels and a fine carriage with the padded interior still intact. Harry was the first to put his head through the handle and grab the sides.

'Right, jump in, Wendy. You're first.' She was hoisted up and onto their new found toy. They set off with Wendy squealing with delight. Harry was pushing with all his might. He knew it would be more fun coming back down the hill. They eventually turned round to face the others who were left down below.

'Don't go fast, Harry!' She was wearing a worried look. 'Don't push too hard!'

'It's OK. We'll manage to stop!' he shouted as they set off. This was a fine machine with well-sprung wheels giving a nice bounce to the journey. Harry had managed about twelve steps when he felt his legs going a little bit faster than they were designed to go. He was clinging on with his feet up on the axle. Wendy was hanging on for dear life, her body bouncing up and down with the motion.

'Look out! They're going to run us over,' Norman shouted. The pram and its occupants hurtled towards them. Harry had his feet on the ground by now, trying to slow down. Had a stranger been watching, they would not have been able to recognise the scene. The pram was lost in a cloud of dust that was coming from his boots which were trailing along the sandy road. Somehow the two of them slowed to a halt twenty yards past the rest of them.

'That was great fun,' said a nearly unrecognisable Harry who was covered in dust from head to toe. Wendy climbed out, helped by Vince.

'You've got to try that,' she said, shivering with excitement.

'We'll all get a go later. Let's get up to Brodie's.' They could hear him with his tractor working somewhere in the top field. They set off with Vince pushing the pram and Norman as a passenger. They stopped for a moment to pick a few summer fruits from the roadside bushes.

Farmer Brodie was gathering the sheaves of wheat which were stacked uniformly throughout the field, all facing a point taken from somewhere in the distant hillside. Mrs Brodie was throwing up the sheaves with a pitchfork to her husband who then arranged them neatly on the cart.

'Hello there,' he shouted from the top, noticing the arrival of four bodies and a pram.

'You come to give us a hand, then?'

'Yes,' they answered in harmony.

'OK, we'll take in this load now. You can help with the next one. Follow us back. Don't stand too close to the trailer.' They followed behind the tractor and its load: Mrs Brodie at the wheel driving slowly, careful not to shed the load, her husband perched on top.

'Right, who's going to throw down the sheaves?'

Harry and Norman were nominated to go up the ladder and on to the top of the load and Wendy and Vince would help Brodie build the stack. Mrs Brodie was off to the farmhouse to put the kettle on and look out the scones that she'd baked.

'Throw them down on the middle now, lads, and we'll build them out.' They soon got the hang of it. They had to throw the sheaves so that they landed on the side of the farmer who then picked them up and laid them down neatly in a circular formation. Wendy and Vince were responsible for the centre of the stack which had to be built up accordingly. Norman was having great fun, throwing the sheaves on to the heads of the two below who were falling over trying to dodge the straw sheaves. When the cart was almost empty, Mrs Brodie had to fork up the last few rounds of sheaves as the lads were now not able to reach the height that Brodie and his helpers were at. When that was completed they all came down the ladder which had been put in place.

'What happens now?'

'We'll top it off with the next load we get. Mother! Where's that tea and scones?'

They set off back to the field, Brodie driving a little faster this time, the rest of them and the dog bouncing about in the empty cart. It was agreed that Wendy and Vince would build up the cart this time with Mrs Brodie forking. After they had loaded up again and on the ride back, the two on top of the cart found that they could reach the branches of the trees. They would hold on to them as long as they could, careful not to pull themselves off the top of the cart. One or two of the branches would sneak up on them and they had to wriggle under to avoid getting knocked off. Back at the farmyard the youngsters stood to one side and left the Brodies to top off the last stack. They drove the tractor and cart forward to start a new stack with Harry and Norman now dodging the sheaves being tossed down. Sometime later they were carted back to the field where they collected the pram for the walk home. It was getting late. They were tired and hungry. The scones had gone down well but they had all worked up a healthy appetite. They agreed that it was just as well that Podge hadn't been there. The rest would have had even less to eat. Norman was in the pram again with Vince pushing. It wasn't long before they had built up some speed. Suddenly, the pram veered right with Vince unable to hold on and steer. Norman was now on his own, thundering down the hill pondering his fate. He headed straight for Patrick's pond and a swear word was heard as he sailed through the air and into the water causing the ducks to scatter. When the rest of them caught up, Norman could be seen, going round in circles, paddling furiously, with his hands.

'Is the pram OK?' someone shouted.

'Never mind the stupid pram. Get me out!' Norman shrieked.

They managed somehow to get him and the pram back on dry land with the aid of some rope they had found. Norman seemed to be alright and they had the added bonus of an undamaged waterproof toy that would double up as a craft of the high seas if the need arose. They were soon home at the supper table, and then off to bed for much needed sleep.

Chapter Five
1965. Grandma Confesses.

'I'm getting old, Vincent,' Grandma said as Vince helped her pour the Guinness from the bottle into a glass. She had become more unsteady on her feet. Her arthritis was evident as she lay in bed and she rarely got up to sit in the chair anymore. She preferred to lie on the bed and listen to her radio. Her appetite wasn't what it had been although she did like the stew that Pamela made, done the Irish way, along with cabbage. She could always find space in her stomach for a glass of stout and there were always a few bottles on standby. Pamela had given up her part-time work at the post office to be at home for Grandma. There was not enough work for her since Mr Jeffries had passed away and his daughter and son-in-law had taken over. The telegram service was hardly used anymore with an increased dependency on the telephone. Grandma had been slowly getting weaker. She'd had a good life and was not a complainer but she knew her time was approaching.

'Vincent, there's something I want to tell you. I've never told anyone else.'

'What is it, Gran?'

'You know your Grandad was in the war?'

'Yes, you've told me lots of times.'

'Well,' she stopped to sip her stout, 'he did something very bad.'

'What! He shot someone?'

'I don't know about that, he never talked much about it. He was in Germany and one day found himself in a building that had been bombed. It could have been a bank, I suppose. Anyway, he was alone for a while, waiting for his unit to catch up, I think. He was looking for booby traps when he found a box. A deposit box or something and inside the box there were bits of metal, or so he thought.' She paused for another sip. 'Where was I?'

'A box, and metal bits.'

'That's right. Your Grandad had a closer look and saw that they were coins,' she paused again.

'What's that? Coins! What kind of coins?'

'They were gold coins.' She stopped for another drink of the stout. 'Are you listening to all of this, Vincent?'

'Yes, Gran.'

'What was I saying?'

'Coins, gold coins.'

'Right, well anyway, he took the coins and put them in his pack. He knew that the Germans would have done the same. He thought that he could always give them back, or so he said. Anyhow, he never told his unit about it and he came back home with them. Get us another bottle, Vincent, and have a glass yourself.'

'What?' Vince was mesmerised with this story.

'Open me another bottle.'

Vince reached inside the cabinet beside the bed and

produced another of her favourite tipple.

'Get a glass for yourself.' She had a twinkle in her eye just like she used to have when Vince listened to all those wonderful stories she told.

'What happened next?'

'I said that he took them home, didn't I?'

'You said that Grandad came home with them.'

'OK, well, he knew that he couldn't do anything about them just then. He would have been in terrible trouble, so he decided to stash them somewhere safe.'

'What, here in the house?'

'No, we didn't live here then. We had a rented place over in the valley.'

'So where did he hide them, then?' Vince was already half-way down his glass.

She leaned closer. 'At Ferguson's place,' she whispered. 'Your Grandad worked at his place when Ferguson's father was alive.' They both stopped for another drink.

'So when did he go back and get them?'

'He didn't. He died before he had the chance to.' She had a sad look in her eyes now. The twinkle had gone.

'What do you mean? He didn't get them back?'

'No.'

'What happened to them?'

'They should still be there.'

'Still there...are they worth a lot of money?'

'I should imagine so.'

'What, even now?'

'They should be worth a lot more now.'

'Is this a true story, Gran?' She had told countless

stories to him before and it didn't matter that some of her tales were a little far-fetched. He was always an eager student.

'Yes, it's true and I want you to find them, Vincent.'

'Bloody hell!'

'Don't use that language here.'

'Sorry.'

'I want you to find them and get money for them.'

'How do I do that?'

'You'll find a way, and when you do, I want you to give the money to your mother and father. Just keep this to yourself.'

Vince had finished his stout and was looking at the empty glass.

'Want another?'

'Yes please. It tastes quite nice.'

'Help yourself, but don't go sneaking into my room just because you're getting a taste for it,' she said with a smile.

'I wouldn't pinch your stout, Gran. Tell me again, you want me to find these...these coins and somehow get them cashed for money?'

'That's right, my boy.'

'Christ!'

'Vincent!'

'Sorry. Where about at Ferguson's place are they hidden?'

'Ah! Your Grandad didn't tell me exactly. What I do know is that they must be in the buildings somewhere. I know he didn't bury them.'

Vince could feel the Guinness going to his head.

'Slow down with that. Stop gulping it.' Vince hadn't realised he had finished the second glassful.

'Nobody else knows about this. I haven't told your mother or father. When I'm gone and if you manage to find the coins, just say that they must have been mine and that I hid them somewhere. You'll think of something.'

'What do they look like?'

'They'll be small in size and have the head of the German ruler Wilhelm. Your Grandad was a good man. I know that he shouldn't have stolen them in the first place but strange things happened then. It wasn't an easy time.'

'How am I going to find these gold coins? I mean, are you saying I can't tell Mum and Dad?'

'Vincent, I'm telling you because if anyone can find them, you can.'

'If they're still there.'

'Yes, if they are still there. You do what you have to. It would be nice if you could find them. Your parents could use the money.'

'And what about you, Gran?'

'Oh, don't worry about me. I have plenty of stout nowadays.' She had finished her drink by now. 'I'm sleepy. This is our secret, remember. Now, off you go. Don't do anything right now. Take your time. Ferguson won't know about this, so you be careful.'

'OK, Gran,' he said, tucking in her cover. 'I'll see you tomorrow. Good night.'

'You are a good lad, Vincent, night, night.'

Vince lay in his bed that night trying to recall all that his Grandma had said. It wasn't long before he was fast asleep aided by the stout he had drunk.

'You're very quiet, Odd Job, you in love or something?'

'Nah, just thinking.' He had woken up that morning wondering if his conversation with his Grandma had been a dream. Then he remembered the stout.

'I had some of Gran's Guinness last night. It tastes OK,' he told Spike on the way to school.

'What did your Dad say?'

'He didn't see me. Anyway, I only had the two glasses. I've had a taste of his beer before, I prefer Gran's stout.'

This was the last week at primary school before the summer holidays began. They all were to move on to the academy after the break. That Tuesday dragged on longer than usual. Vince quickly changed into his old clothes that day.

'Can I have my supper now, Mum?'

'What's your hurry, Vincent? Your Dad will be home shortly, you'll just have to wait. Go and see your Grandma while I get the table set.'

'Hello, Gran. How are you feeling today?' She was lying on the bed drifting in and out of sleep. The radio was still on.

'Switch that thing off, will you, Vincent. Have you come for more of my stout?'

'Just checking to see how you are. Can I get you anything? Tea's about ready.'

'I'm not very hungry. Have you been thinking about what we talked about last night?'

'Yes, Gran, I'll tell you if I find anything out. You don't want me to tell anyone, do you?'

'Not unless you have to. Trust me. It's better if you don't.'

'OK.'

'Supper's ready! Your Dad's home,' shouted Pamela. 'Is Grandma wanting some stew?'

'Tell your Mum I'll just have a cup of tea.'

'I'll bring it through, Gran, and a biscuit.'

'Have you decided what you're going to do in the holidays, Vince, you've only three days to go?'

'No, not really, Dad. I thought I would ask Mr Ferguson if he needed any help on the farm.'

'What's the matter, have you fallen out with Brodie?'

'Nah, we can give him a hand as well.'

'You can start by cleaning out the shed. I can't get moved in there because of all your rubbish.'

Vince finished the stew. 'I'll tidy it, I promise. I must run. I said I would meet Norman.'

'What are you two doing this evening then?' asked Mrs Halford as she met Vince at her front door.

'We're just out on the bikes for a while.'

'I'll race you!' shouted Norman as the two of them set off down the road, weaving from side to side.

'Right, first one to Ferguson's place.' Vince was thinking hard. Norman got there first as he had a better bike. Vince could see Ferguson's tractor and cart in the field that ran beside the main road.

'C'mon, Norman. Let's see what he's doing.' Vince was first to the dykeside. Ferguson was checking that the water trough for his cattle was working.

'Hello, Mr Ferguson.'

'How are you lads doing? School holidays yet?'

'No, next week.'

'You'll be looking for that young girl from Ardrossan, I suppose. I haven't heard if the family are coming this year. Have you?'

'No, I don't think so. There's been no word,' replied Vince.

'Doesn't she write to you? I thought you two were in love. I was going to clean out the caravan just in case. I might get somebody at the last minute. Best be prepared.'

'Do you need a hand with it?'

'Well, if you've nothing better to do. I'm not paying money, though.'

'That's OK. We'll do it for nothing. We've plenty of time in the holidays.'

'That's settled then. You come up past the house anytime and I'll get you started.'

'Is next week OK?'

'Fine, you lads just pop in past.'

'Right, last one back is a big girl's blouse.'

They raced back down to the houses. Norman was doing fine until his bike chain came off.

'Bugger! I meant to tighten it earlier.'

'Come on, we'll walk the rest.'

'Are you serious about Ferguson's caravan?'

'Yeah.'

'What are you up to?'

'If I tell you, you have to keep it a secret.'

'I will.'

'You have to promise or I'll kick your arse!'

'Sure, I promise. What is it?'

Vince told Norman the story about his Grandad and

by the time that he had finished they were back outside Norman's house.

'Bloody hell! You think all this is true?'

'Yes, Gran wouldn't lie about something like that. Do you want to help me find these coins?'

'Yeah, great.'

'You've not to tell Spike or the rest of them. We'll have a look around next week, they must be somewhere.'

'OK, OK, I'll see you at school tomorrow. Three more days till the holidays...great!'

'Well, where have you and Norman been?' asked Pamela.

'We were talking to Mr Ferguson. He needs his caravan spruced up. We said we'd give him a hand.'

'You'll tidy the shed first, OK?'

'I said I would, Dad. I'll do it at the weekend.'

'Did Ferguson say if Julie and her parents were coming this year?'

'He didn't think so. They haven't been in touch.'

Pamela gave him a comforting smile. 'Shame, I'd have liked to have seen the little darling again. She's such a sensible girl.'

'Not so little,' thought Vince.

'Well, we'll just have to wait and see. Have you any homework to do?'

'No, I won't have any more to do now. Miss Holby said we would get a half-day on Friday.'

'Will you miss her, Vincent?'

'Yes, she's been OK.' He would miss the bicycle shed too.

The Friday came and went. There were some prizes to

be given out with Podger receiving a special book for being a clever clogs. They all said their goodbyes to Miss Holby. There was a slight moistening of her eyes but she held up well.

'Did you say goodbye to everyone, Vincent?'

'No need to, I'll see them all at the academy anyway.'

'Right, my boy, you're coming into town with me. You're getting a haircut. Look at the state of you.'

'Aw, Mum!'

'Don't *Aw Mum* me. It's either the barber shop or your Dad will use the clippers again.'

'What about Gran? We can't leave her on her own.'

'She's not being left on her own. I've arranged with Norman's Mum to come over and sit with her.'

'Can Norman come with us?'

'I don't see why not. You run over and tell Mrs Halford we're ready. We can catch the two o'clock bus if you hurry.'

Vince was back with Norman and his Mum after telling Norman, 'It's bloody haircut time again.'

Norman was chuckling to himself. He knew how Odd Job hated having his hair cut, especially when his Dad did it. He had a tendency to overdo things.

'I don't know what you're laughing at, Norman. You can go and get a haircut too. Here, this should be enough and I want some change.'

'But Mum, we're wanting our hair to grow longer. It's the fashion. Everyone will laugh at us.'

'You're about to start the holidays, who's going to notice you apart from your chums. Anyway, it will soon grow. Now stop arguing. You'll have Mrs Wright missing her bus.'

The two lads crept out of the barber's shop that afternoon agreeing that they would have to lie low for a few days. They were not wearing that balaclava again. They were too old for that.

'You can help me clear the shed out tomorrow. It'll keep my Dad happy,' Vince said to Norman.

'When are we going to Ferguson's?'

'We can go on Monday. He said just to go round, didn't he?'

They crouched low in the bus on the journey back: one baldie reading *The Topper*, the other, *The Dandy*. Pamela had bought a new coat at the sales. She was fed up going to church in the tatty, old, grey one. She was happy that this new one was fawn-coloured, it would go with her skirt and blouse. By half past four they were back home. Spike was leaning on his bike talking to Wendy as they stepped off the bus.

'Nice haircut, lads, are you both joining the army?'

'Yeah, we're getting guns and bayonets and we're going to stick them up your arse!'

'Vincent! Do you have to talk like that? In front of Wendy too!'

'Sorry, Mum.'

'I'm going to let Norman's Mum get home. Don't be late. Tea will be about an hour.'

'Bye, Mrs Wright. Vince, I think your hair looks nice. It makes you two look older.'

'Thank you, Wendy. What are you two doing this week-end?' Vince asked Spike. 'Me and Norman are cleaning out Dad's shed. You can help if you like.'

'No thanks, I've better things to do,' replied Spike.

'I'll help if it's OK,' said Wendy. 'I've to sort out the hymn books with my Dad but that won't take long.'

'OK, just come round past. I'm off for something to eat.'

'Are you coming out tonight, Odd Job?' asked Spike.

'Naw, I'm going to watch *Steptoe and Son.*'

'Did you see it last week?'

'Yeah, I watched it with Dad. He never misses it... *Harold!*'

'I'm off, see you tomorrow.'

*

Vince was up early that Saturday and was quickly joined by Norman.

'Right, where do we start?'

'Dunno, I'll ask Dad.' He left Norman pottering about in the shed and was back a few minutes later with instructions.

'Dad says that we've to tidy up my stuff and put the garden tools in one place. We have to clear up those boxes and wood as well. Let's put everything outside then we'll sweep up.'

Wendy arrived to lend a hand and was quickly nominated as sweep. Vince was careful not to throw out his bike spares. They had the contents of the shed piled up in the garden and by lunchtime it was back inside with little or no difference whatsoever. Matthew came round for the inspection and found them sitting on the ground beside the empty boxes.

'Have you thrown anything out at all? What about all that junk of yours, Vincent?'

'It's not junk, Dad. That's spares for my bike.'
'Get it thrown out now. I want to see those boxes full.'
'Aw, OK.'

They managed to fill two boxes, mostly with wood. He wasn't going to throw away everything. 'Never know when I might need that,' he muttered.

'Are we having soup today, Mum? Can Wendy and Norman have as well?'

'Help yourself. I'm going to check on your Gran. I've sent for the doctor. She's not eating very much. Come in and see her before you all go and play.'

Vince and the other two finished their soup. He said he would meet them outside the post office. He just wanted to pop into Grandma's room. She was asleep as he entered. Her breathing was very shallow.

'Gran, Gran, are you asleep?' he asked, holding her hand. She half opened her eyes and gave him a smile. 'She'll feel better tomorrow,' he thought, closing the door quietly. The doctor had just arrived as he was reaching for his bike.

'She's OK, isn't she, Mum? Just tired?'

'You go on and meet your chums. The doctor will see that she's fine.'

Vince caught up with Norman. Harry had joined him. Wendy had gone off home.

'Right, are we off on the bikes then?'

They set off down the road with Vince in front. He led them along the route to Ferguson's fields, stopping at the big tree at the roadside.

'Harry, remember when we climbed this and you fell on the cow shite?'

'Yeah, I remember.'

'Let's climb it.' The trio settled on the branch that offered the best view. Vince was still thinking hard.

'Is Julie coming up this year?' asked Harry as he looked over at the caravan.

'I don't know, I haven't heard,' muttered Vince. His mind was somewhere else. Norman was keeping very quiet. He didn't want to say anything in case he gave something away. He too was sharing the same thoughts as Vince.

'Doesn't she write?'

'What!'

'Julie, doesn't she write you?' Harry could see that Odd Job was miles away.

'Eh, no, she doesn't. She has my address, but she'll have lots of friends.'

'Maybe she has a new boyfriend,' teased Harry.

'Yeah, yeah, maybe.' Vince was wishing that Harry would stop jabbering on. He had more important things to think about. 'Why couldn't he be as quiet as Norman?'

'C'mon, let's get back.'

Vince arrived at his house door just as the Reverend Calder was leaving. 'He must have had a drink from Dad's bottle,' he thought to himself. He could smell the whisky as they passed in the hallway.

'I'll look in again tomorrow, Mrs Wright.'

'Thank you, minister.'

'How's Gran, Mum?'

'Go in and see her but don't wake her. She's very weak.'

Grandma died peacefully in her sleep that night.

Pamela had gone to check on her early in the morning and had found her. At first glance she thought she was asleep, but as she reached out and touched Grandma's hand, she found that she was cold. Pamela woke Matthew and Vince after she had called for the doctor. Vince was asked to go round to Norman's until the doctor and the minister had been to make the arrangements for the funeral. The Reverend would call the undertaker first thing in the morning and the service was to be held on the Wednesday at the local church. The house was bustling with people coming and going that afternoon and it was a very tired family that went to sleep that night. The undertaker arrived on the Monday morning with the coffin. Grandma's remains were to lie in her room until the service on Wednesday. Vince went through with his Dad to the room in which his Gran was lying in her coffin. She looked so peaceful and somehow she looked younger with hardly any of the wrinkles that were part of her features. Neighbours came to offer their condolences and many cups of tea were drunk. Pamela insisted that Matthew go to his work as normal because he would have the whole of Wednesday off. There was no need for him to be at home on the Monday and Tuesday as she had plenty to occupy her time with all the people coming round past the house.

On the day of the service, Vince helped to carry the coffin the short distance to the graveyard and was given a cord. He listened to what his Dad said about the procedure and was careful not to wrap the cord round his hand at the graveside. Grandma was laid to rest beside her husband who had died all those years earlier. The funeral party was invited for tea and sandwiches back at the pub. George and Betty were rushed off their feet that day. It wasn't long before the black ties were discarded along with the jackets. Most of the funeral party stayed until closing time with the Reverend Calder being one of the last to leave the building. He was eager to join in the sing-song after a few gin and tonics.

*

The family household was getting back to normal by the Friday. Vince had helped his Mum clear out Grandma's room. They had washed the bedding and gathered up her few precious belongings along with some bottles of Guinness.

'Can I have one please, Mum?'

'Alright, but take it to your room. Don't let your father catch you. We'll put the rest through in the cabinet.'

'Can I go and see Norman now? I told him I would be over.'

'Go on then. Don't be late for supper.'

He found Norman adjusting the brakes on his bike.

'Are you about finished? I thought we would go to Ferguson's.'

They mounted up and set off on the first phase of their mission. Ferguson was loading a cattle trough on to his tractor and cart.

'Hello, lads. Have you two come to help me then? I was sorry to hear about your Grandma, Vince. Your Grandfather worked here at one time helping my father. Did you know that?'

'I think Grandma might have mentioned it. What did he do anyway?'

'Oh, he did various jobs around the place, doing this and that. I remember him well, a good worker. He could lend his hand to anything.'

Ferguson had been left to carry on farming the land after his father died. His mother had lived on a few years more but now he was the last in line. He was an only child and he had never married. Some said he was too miserable to share his meagre existence, with anyone.

'Where do you want us to start? You mentioned the caravan.'

'That's right, it needs cleaning out. I've got some of my bee stuff inside and it needs washing down. Come on I'll show you.'

They wandered over to the caravan, opened the door and were greeted by stacks of beekeeping equipment still covered in the left over bees' wax.

'You can scrape off the wax and scrub the frames. I'll get some brushes and water. Stack them over there when you get them clean. You'll have the floor of the van to clean as well. Think you can manage that?'

'Yuk! Yeah we'll manage.'

Ferguson came back from the house with a pail of hot water, scraper and brush. 'I'm going to leave you two to get on with it. I have to get this trough up to the field.'

'Leave it to us, Mr Ferguson. You go ahead with your work.'

The boys set about the cleaning. First they scraped the frames used in the bee hives. Then they used the wire brush before washing the frames down with water. Ferguson was well away by this time. They could hear him making his way to the far field.

'Right, let's have a look around.' The two of them wandered over to the outbuilding. The door they opened was the one that led through the barn and into the court where the cattle spent the winter months. The muck had been cleaned out earlier in the year but there was still the smell of cow manure. They went through another door, past the crusher for the turnips and up the wooden steps to where the barley was stored after harvest time.

'Bloody hell! This place smells.'

'Too right, let's go back and check that other door.'

They made their way back outside into the fresh air and tried the other door. It was a bit stiff but with a good shove, it was open.

'Blimey! Look at the stuff in here.'

The building was full of old junk and horse tackle and had an old and musty smell to it.

'Hurry up!' Vince shouted to Norman who was having a rummage around in an old chest. 'We'd better get back to the cleaning.'

'Your Grandad could have hidden the coins anywhere. Where are we supposed to look?'

'There's one more shed. Hurry up, let's see what's inside.' The door to the shed that was used to store the firewood was already half open.

'What are you lads up to?' They hadn't heard Ferguson come back. He had stopped his tractor round the other side of the house.

'Sorry, Mr Ferguson. We were just exploring.'

'Well, that's OK. Just be careful. I have some sharp and dangerous stuff lying around. I wouldn't want you to hurt yourselves. Do you see that shed over there?' He pointed to the one that held the junk. 'That's where your Grandfather spent a lot of his time. My father had horses in those days and your Grandfather would groom them and look after the tackle. I'll show you.' They went inside for the second time. 'Of course, all this stuff wasn't here then. It just seems to accumulate. I need to have a clean out sometime.'

'We can help you.'

'How are you getting on with the caravan?'

'It's taking a while to get those frames clean. Can we do a bit more then come back another time?'

'Just come past whenever you like. I'll leave the key in the van door. You can get water from the tap over there.' He pointed to the stand pipe in the corner of the wall. 'It'll be cold but you can manage without hot, can't you?'

'Yes, easily.' Vince was trying to take in all that he could see before him. 'Bloody hell,' he thought. 'If the coins are in here, they could be any place. Where do we start?'

'Well, I'll leave you lads to finish up. Just leave the key in the door. Remember what I said.'

'OK, we'll carry on a bit longer. C'mon, Norman, let's get to it and then we'll get home for tea.' They scraped and scrubbed for another ten minutes but soon got fed up.

'What do you think then?' Norman asked.

'I think we should pack it in for today. We know the layout now. We'll have to keep coming back. I'd like to have a good look in that shed over there. Let's get home and change. My feet are wet.'

'OK, I'll race you back.'

The two of them jumped on their bikes and set off.

The first week of the holidays passed. Vince had been helping out at home. Pamela insisted that he lend a hand with the various duties around the house and garden. Norman had called in past to escape the drudgery. He too had been helping his Mum with similar duties. The rest of the gang were absent presumably having been captured by their respective parents and commandeered to do their bit as well.

'Mum, me and Norman said we'd go back to Ferguson's to finish his caravan. He must be wondering where we've got to. Can we go tomorrow? I've done the garden.'

'Yes, OK. You've been a help. Just chop up some firewood to keep your Dad happy and you can go and see Norman.'

'Thanks Mum.'

The firewood was done and Vince was now knocking on Norman's door. 'Hello, Mrs Halford. Can Norman come out tomorrow?'

'I suppose so. You'll be wanting to get up to some mischief no doubt. I'll tell him to come over for you after breakfast.'

'Thanks.'

The next morning they were eager and ready and by nine o'clock they were at the door of the caravan. Ferguson was nowhere to be seen so they went to the shed where the outside tap was.

'Look at this mess. Where will we start looking?'

'There's only four or five chests. That shouldn't take long. We'll have to climb over the rest of this junk to get to them all. We'd better finish the bee stuff first. Where do you suppose he is anyway?'

They scraped and washed and were just about finished when the farmer returned in his Land Rover.

'Hello, lads, I wondered when you'd would be back. How are you getting on?'

'We're just about finished. Are these frames OK?'

'You've made a fine job of them, saved me a lot of work. What do you want to do now?'

'We thought we could help clean out that shed,' replied Vince, pointing to the one that held their fascination.

'Well, alright then. You just do that. You can sort all that horse tackle and stack those chests on top of one another. If I had more space to move about in there it would be better.'

'We'll get started then. We have to go home for our dinner soon. Is it OK if we come back in the afternoon?'

'Of course, I have to be away till teatime so you two just carry on. I might see you later.'

Ferguson went away leaving Norman and Vince the freedom of the farm. They pulled out two of the biggest chests to allow them some working space and then they set about gathering up the leather tackle that had once been an integral part of farming life. They emptied the two chests that held nothing more than bits and pieces of old hand tools and torn sacks.

They stopped working to cycle home for something to eat and by half-past one they were back at the shed. Most of the shed contents were outside by now. They found a couple of brushes to sweep the concrete floor. The dust that resulted in the sweeping had them coughing so they went exploring while it settled. They went back into the barn and cattle court which still had the horrible smell. They checked upstairs to where the barley was kept, taking time to look in every dark corner. Norman shifted some potato bags and the balls of twine that were needed for the machine used to bale the straw.

'There's nothing that could be hidden in here. Have we checked everywhere?'

'Yup, we've covered every corner twice, haven't we? Let's get some fresh air. This is horrible.'

'Is this floor solid?'

'Yes, I've checked, and the upstairs floor as well.'

'What's that in the rafters? Is it a bird's nest?'

'It's a swallow's nest. Haven't you noticed them flying about?'

'Maybe we should ask them if they've seen anything.'

'Very funny, let's get out of here.' They walked round the buildings just to make sure they had been through all the doors. The tractor and cart were kept in the Dutch barn. Nothing could be concealed there as it had a corrugated roof with no sides to it. By the time they returned to the shed the dust had settled, making it more comfortable to get on with the tidying up. They started on the remaining chests which they emptied and stacked. The horse tackle was hung from the various nails that had been hammered into the wooden rafters. Vince stopped for a moment to admire the brass buckles that had at one time been polished with pride.

'I'll bet your Grandad looked after these by polishing them every day. Look at the shine you get when you rub them.' Norman had been rubbing a brass buckle with a piece of sacking, breathing on it to get the right effect. Vince was looking at the inside of the building. The walls were built of big stones but now the masonry in between was crumbling in places. Some of the stones had lines scratched on them where someone had been counting sacks.

'Look! Somebody's drawn a four-leafed clover.'

'That's not a four-leafed clover, Odd Job, that's a shamrock.'

'I knew that.'

'Your Grandad must have done it.'

'Very artistic, it must run in the family.'

'Since when have you been artistic? Your drawings are shite.'

'Oh, you think so. What's this then?' Vince picked up a rusty nail and drew on one of the stones.

'It's the letter W,' said Norman.

'Naw, it's Julie's boobies.'

'Is she coming this year, do you think?'

'You heard what Ferguson said. He doesn't know. If she is, the caravan's nice and clean.'

'It would be nice if she came back, we could all go to the pond again. Do you want to go and smell the bedding? That small mattress must be hers.'

'Bugger off,' replied Vince, throwing a dirty sack over his chum.

'I challenge you to a duel.' Norman picked up the brush and the two of them engaged in mortal combat. They left some of the rubbish outside the shed, not knowing what Ferguson wanted to do with it. Next morning they cycled back to show him their day's work.

'We haven't had a look in that shed that holds the firewood,' Norman had mentioned on the way there.

'You're right. It isn't very big. We'll have a look when we get the chance.'

'Morning, Mr Ferguson.' He was mending a wooden gate that was past its best.

'Fine job you did again, lads.'

'We left that lot of stuff outside. We didn't know what to do with it.'

'I'll see if Patrick will give me a few shillings for it. It's no use to me,' said Ferguson.

'What about your wood shed? You want us to tidy it up?'

'Please yourselves. There's not much to tidy up, but go ahead.'

'OK, we'll have a look.'

The wood shed was the smallest. As well as the logs there were a few old biscuit tins full of nuts and bolts that the farmer would search out when his machinery was in need of repair. It took the two of them an hour to clean and sweep it out. They had a close inspection of the shed and established that there was nothing hidden in there. Ferguson came over with two mugs of tea.

'Here you are. Well, I've never seen the place look so tidy. You boys should go into business together when you leave school.'

'Aw, it's nothing. We like to keep busy.'

'Look, I feel I should be paying you something but you know how it is, things are tight.'

'It's alright, we don't need paid.'

'How about helping me take this stuff over to

Patrick's?'

Ferguson and the lads loaded the bits of scrap and old tools on to the cart and jumped on board with the farmer at the wheel of his tractor. It didn't take them long to make the short journey to the blacksmith. The remains of the raft could still be seen, floating in the reeds as they passed the duck pond.

Patrick was repairing a shaft for a plough, hammering away with beads of sweat dripping from his forehead. His dog rose from its sleep, ambled over to meet them, made its statement then went back to the filthy tarpaulin it had been lying on.

'Hello there, Patrick,' said Ferguson.

'Whad ye want?' Patrick was now busy trying to analyse the mass that he had just extracted from his nose.

'I've some scrap in the cart. I want to see what it's worth.'

'Scrap isn't worth a shite these days.' Patrick was now rolling his meal on his trouser leg. He went over and had a quick look in the back of the cart.

'I'll give you five bob for it.'

'But there's a piece of lead there, that's worth more.'

'Isn't worth a shite. Five bob. Take it or leave it.'

'Fair enough. Five shillings it is. Lads, can you throw that stuff off?'

Patrick reached into his pocket and came up with two half-crowns for the deal.

'I've a set of discs that need some welding done sometime.'

'Bring it over.' He turned back to his plough repair. One hand had a spanner in it, the other had disappeared up his nose.

'Well, lads, thanks again for your help.' The three of them arrived back at the farm with Norman and Vince having discussed the day's proceedings in the back of the cart.

'What do we do now, Odd Job?'

'Dunno. We've seen everything. Maybe these coins don't exist.'

'But your Gran said.'

'Yeah, I know. Let's go home.'

'Where have you two been?' said Podger, arriving with Spike. Podger was almost finished his jam sandwich. He had met up with Spike earlier on.

'We've been helping Ferguson.'

'Doing what?'

'Oh, tidying up at his place.'

'Did he pay you anything?'

'Naw, we were bored. We did it for nothing.'

'You're bloody stupid.'

'Well, anyway, you know he's a skinflint.'

'We wondered where you two had got to. Did Ferguson say if Julie was coming up this year?'

'He wasn't sure. There's been no word. What have you been doing?' asked Vince.

'Apart from helping out at home, nothing really,' replied Podger.

'How about we go into town sometime? I know my Mum and Dad will let me. What about you lot?'

'Good idea, Spike. We can go on Saturday. Are we all on for it?'

The four of them nodded in agreement, knowing they

would have to check the cash reserves first.

*

Matthew drove them into town that weekend with the agreement that they would catch the teatime bus home. They were all growing up fast. They wanted some amount of independence extended to them. This was granted by the parents on certain conditions. Over the coming weeks and months there was a lot of give and take from both sides. The trips to town were always looked forward to. They could wander round the shops imagining all the clothes that they would buy when they had the money. Going to Simpson Reid the music store was a firm favourite. They could go to the record booth and request a record to be played. They didn't have to buy it there and then. They could only afford to purchase one on a very rare occasion. The youngsters depended on the radio to stay in touch with the expanding pop scene. The visits to Simpson Reid's offered the opportunity for them to pretend to be pop stars. The instruments were grabbed by eager hands. Spike always wanted to be Elvis, the others, a mixture of Cliff or Marty Wilde or Hank Marvin. They were asked on more than one occasion to leave the instruments alone, particularly when Podger got behind one of the drum kits. He wasn't prepared to mime like the rest of them who had the guitars. He had to have a whack on the snare drum and a crash on the symbols. It was usually at this point that they were asked to leave.

'Come on, Ringo, let's get something to eat,' they would offer the dejected, potential superstar.

'How are you supposed to learn if they keep stopping you?'

'I think you're meant to buy the kit first, Podge.'
'Some bloody chance of that,' he replied.

They would sometimes go in past the café just off the High Street to have a Coke and play the jukebox. Antonio's was a favourite stopping off place for the gang. Podger had to have a sticky bun if he could afford it. If he didn't have the cash, he could usually persuade Susan to hand one over with the promise that he would pay next time. Susan worked in the café that was owned by the Italian descendant. She was older than the assembled gang but that did not stop the Berrydale lot from flicking their straws at her to get some attention. There would sometimes be quite a battle in the café with straws flying about in all directions unless Antonio was there on one of his rare visits. He much rather preferred to swan about in his Alfa Romeo than do a day's work. Susan was perfectly happy to run things on her own although she did have to remind Antonio when they were running low on the home-made ice cream. The lads were filling up with testosterone as well as Coca Cola. There were many discussions that summer about their spreading body hair. They had to have a routine check at bed time to see what was happening down and around their new found friend. The girls were also having the experience of impending puberty with the addition of having to keep an eye on what was going on around the chest area. They would look in the mirror every night from every angle. There was definitely something about to happen. It was the first topic of conversation whenever they met up for a girlie chat. All the young Berrydale women would soon be catching up with Julie from Ardrossan. The thought of gold war coins had been put on hold for the time being. Norman and Vince spoke about it briefly once or twice but they were no further forward. They all made a few visits up to Brodie's to help with his farming jobs and to stock up with the wild fruit pickings at the side of the road when time allowed. One particularly hot day, they used Patrick's pond to cool off. He was away somewhere for the whole day and they enjoyed uninterrupted play with only the ducks as bystanders.

The summer wore on. Parents had to make the journey to town to kit out their children with the uniform required for the academy. Hair had to be cut again. This time Matthew had insisted that he did it himself using the clippers. He'd spent enough money on the blazer, trousers and shoes and he wasn't about to give unnecessary money to the barber shop when he could make just as good a job of the trimming himself. Vince would be glad to get that first week past with, to give his thatch a chance to recover from the brutal treatment. Spike had somehow managed to retain most of his hair intact and was quick to remind the others of their bald appearance. Spike had managed to acquire a pair of sunglasses to add to his appearance. He seemed to be going through a Roy Orbison phase. It was a pity that he couldn't get the voice right. He was not a singer but that did not prevent him from making a fool of himself. He was convinced that when he left school he was going to be a pop star or an actor and be adored by fans. Spike was already practising his signature in preparation for the time when he would be inundated by girls for his autograph. The scrawled name would have to be short and easy to write. He wouldn't get a lot of time with the girls chasing him and trying to tear his clothes off. He had decided that he would stay in the best hotels rather than buy a mansion. That would prevent all of his adoring fans from defacing his property. Spike had read about what John, Paul, George and Ringo had to put up with and look what had happened to his pal's property in Memphis. 'I'll phone Graceland and have a chat with Elvis after my first single comes out,' he mused to himself. 'Christ! I'm going to need a manager as well.'

Chapter Six
1965-1968. The Academy Years.

Lucy had missed the first two weeks of the new school. She had been in bed with the measles. She arrived with the others on the bus and caused quite a stir as she strutted into the academy. Her skirt was shorter than most of the other girls and she revelled in the attention she was commanding as she made her way to the morning assembly. At the first break, Wendy approached.

'Well, what do you think?' she asked.

'It's alright, a bit different from Berrydale Junior, lots more boys here. Have you found a boyfriend yet?'

'No, don't be silly. How do you manage to wear such a short skirt. Do your Mum and Dad not mind?'

'Look, I'll show you.' Lucy lifted her jumper and unrolled her skirt down from the waist. 'This is for home.' She rolled it up again. 'And this is for school. Now you do it.' Wendy took hold of her waistband and rolled it over and over until the skirt was above her knees. A passing boy gave her a wolf whistle.

'See, just remember to put it back before you go home and also, the next time you are in the Art class, pinch some charcoal and I'll show you how to do your eyes.'

This was another practice that was quickly adopted by the girls. They were quick to catch on that if they wore a bra they would get the attention of the boys who would love to ping the back strap in the passing. Their Mums took a lot of convincing that they needed to wear one whether they could fill it or not. 'I need it for sports, Mum,' was a popular excuse. One day, Wendy had forgotten to remove her charcoal make-up before she arrived home and had to suffer the wrath of the Reverend Calder who sent her off to bed early after making her read a passage from the New Testament. She made a mental note to be much more careful from then on. 'I get enough of this at Sunday School,' she thought. Her Mum could only look on in sympathy. She had done a similar thing with charcoal on the back of her legs all those years before.

*

Vince noticed her in the playground at the morning break. He had passed her before between classes in the corridor. She was in 3A along with Podger. Her hair was long and blonde, almost hiding her pretty face.

'What's her name, Podge?'

'Who?'

'Her...the one with the blonde hair.'

'Alexandria, Alex. Why? Do you fancy her then?'

'Has she got a boyfriend?'

'Dunno, she's quieter than most in our class.'

'Do you think she'll be at the record hop on Saturday?'

'Why? Are we going?'

'Might as well. I've got some money for the bus and the chips. How about you?'

'Yeah, I've got some money.'

'Alex, come here will you?' Podger shouted. She stopped talking to her friend and walked over to where the two were standing.

'Odd Job was wondering if you were going to the hop on Saturday?'

She blushed. 'I might be.'

'Are you going with anyone?'

'Just my friend...why?'

'Go on, Odd Job. Ask her.'

'Hello, I was wondering if you would be there...cos we'll probably go...I thought...I mean, if I ask for a dance, I thought...'

'Yes,' she answered, helping him with his awkwardness.

'Great, we'll see you there.'

'OK, I'll look out for you. Bye,' Alex said, tilting her head and smiling with her eyes.

The record hop was held once a month. It was a handy place to meet girls. Two of the older schoolboys were in charge of things. They would take it turn to change the records on the turntable of the Dansette.

That Saturday it was raining as they ran for the bus. Podger was last to the bus stop, catching up with Vince, Norman and Spike. They had asked Wendy but the Reverend Calder had put his foot down. Harry was also absent. He had spent all of his pocket money and was sulking in front of the TV. Lucy arrived just as the bus pulled up. She wouldn't have missed this for the world. The young vamp had a lot of dancing to look forward to. The word had got around at school that Lucy was going to the hop. The boys would be there in the hope that they might be afforded a dance.

'Who's got the ciggies?'

Spike pulled out a ten of Senior Service and they lit up as they started the journey to town on the back seat of the bus. Podger was admiring the skirt that Lucy was almost wearing.

'Are you wearing drawers?' he asked.

'Mind your own bloody business!' was the reply. It was a stupid question anyway. Her blue skirt did nothing to hide her knickers. The choice was white tonight.

'I've got a hanky that's bigger than that dress.'

'I'm not surprised, Spike, considering the size of your nose.'

Dancing at the record hop was well under way with a good crowd in the hall that served as a meeting place for the youngsters. The Searchers were playing on the Dansette when Vince noticed Alex standing talking to her friend.

'Hello.'

'Hello, yourself.' The make-up that Alex was wearing made her look older than her classroom appearance. She too, had on a very short skirt.

'Want to dance?' Vince asked Alex.

'Yeah, sure.'

'I wasn't interrupting was I?'

'No, my friend Margaret was just keeping me company.'

The Searchers were singing about needles and pins. Alex and Vince were soon doing a version of the Funky Chicken. Spike was having a good look round at the girls. Norman and Podger were deep in conversation.

'Fancy a Coke?' Vince asked.

'Yes, I have money.'

'It's OK, Alex, I'll get them.'

'Are you buying me one as well?' Spike had ambled over to see what was going on.

'I suppose so.'

'We've had a dance. Seen anyone you fancy?'

'Still looking.' Spike was wearing the Beatles style jacket that he was so proud of, the one with the round collar and brass-looking buttons.

'Right, I'm off for a browse. Are you two going to the chipper later?'

'Dunno,' replied Vince, looking hopefully at Alex. 'Where do you live anyway?'

'Just off the High Street. You can catch the bus round the corner from my house if you like,' Alex replied. 'You can walk me home to my house later...if you want to?'

They drank the Cokes. One of Cliff's songs was on the record player. It was a slow one. The two went back on the floor and Alex put her arms round Vince's neck. Their cheeks met as he snuggled into her long blonde hair. He was lost in a world of music and hair when the fight broke out. Two lads had been making fun of Norman's deafness. Spike lashed out at one of them, knocking him sprawling into the table that was being used to stack the 45s. The other lout had produced a flick knife and was circling Spike. 'Come on then. The two of you,' Spike challenged.

'Alex, you wait here.' Vince ran through the crowd of dancers. He grabbed the one with the knife from behind and wrestled him to the floor. Spike was prancing about with a new bravado while the two older and bigger boys who were in charge for the night, stepped in to stop the showdown.

'Let's get out of here,' said Vince, grabbing Alex by the hand. Spike, Norman and Podger followed.

'Are we going to the chipper then? What about you, Alex?'

'No, not for me. You all go.'

'Look, you lot carry on. Me and Alex are going to walk to her house. The last bus is at half-past ten. I'll get on at the stop in the High Street. Get me a bag of chips, will you?'

'What about Lucy?' asked Podger.

'She's still dancing. She can take care of herself. I'll nip back inside and tell her where we are,' said Spike. He found Lucy on the floor during a slow dance. She was wrapped around some fellow whose face had the appearance of having had all his birthdays and a couple of Christmas days land on the same three minutes. Spike told Lucy of the plan of action and left to join the others outside. They broke up to go their separate ways. The lads headed for the chipper with Podger in the lead and Alex and Vince heading in the opposite direction. They stopped in a shop doorway not wishing to get to her house too quickly. They had run out of conversation and were hesitant as to their next move. Vince put his arm around her and they kissed. It was a different kiss to the one he had experienced with Julie. Alex had her mouth open and her tongue was doing strange things to his. He interpreted this as a signal to go exploring and ventured his hand into her blouse.

'I'm not like that!' she snapped, pulling his hand away.

'Sorry.'

'It's OK. Don't do it again.'

'What did this sign with the tongue mean?' he thought. 'Was she just another tease?'

'We'd better get moving. It's going to rain.' They walked to her door and kissed again.

'Can we go out again?' Vince asked eagerly.

'I'd like to,' said Alex.

'What's your last name?'

'Alexander.'

'What, Alexandria Alexander?'

'Yes, what's wrong with that?'

'Nothing.'

'You'd better get going. You'll miss your bus. I'll see you at school.'

'OK, goodnight.'

'Bye.'

Vince only had a few minutes to wait at the stop before the bus came. Spike and the rest of them, apart from Podger, were in the back seat eating their suppers. Podger had finished his double portion and was looking around for seconds. He was trying to sneak a chip from anywhere he could. Lucy was on the same bus, having met up with them outside the chipper. She had left a trail of broken hearts outside the hall and was now feeding her face along with the rest of them.

'Bugger off, Podge! You shouldn't have guzzled yours so fast.'

'Did you get me some chips?'

'Here, Odd Job. They're still hot.'

Vince started eating the chips, taking care not to sit too close to the fat one. He was quite hungry after his date with the beautiful Alex with the long, blonde hair.

'Well, come on Odd Job, how did you get on?'

'Did you put salt and vinegar on these?'

'Yes, yes...Well?'

'Great, she kisses with her tongue. Christ, you know what that means.'

'Did you get a feel?'

'Could have done with more salt.'

'Well...did you?'

'Naw, I'll wait till next time. Guess what her last name is?'

'It's Alexander,' piped up Podger. 'It's Alexander.'

'What, Alexandria Alexander,' laughed Spike.

'Yup.'

'You're joking.'

'Naw, that's her name.'

'Odd Job Wright and Double Sandy. What a couple.'

They were still laughing when they reached their stop.

*

The class had heard about it, had spoken about it and now here it was being brandished by a rather angry Mr Noble. Vince hadn't done his homework and had not been able to answer a question about The French Revolution. It was his second reprimand about the subject and now he stood before the History teacher with his hand held out.

'Which hand do you write with, boy?'

'This one, Sir,' he replied, offering the same hand.

'Then hold out the other one.'

Vince did as he was told and with a resounding whack the first blow was struck. It was to be one of six from the black piece of leather split half-way down the middle. He was sent back to his desk wanting to cry with the pain of it but he managed to hold back his tears. His hand throbbed. He could clearly see the red marks which he would bear for a couple of days.

'Stupid, bloody French Revolution,' he thought, 'why can't they ask about The Lone Ranger and Tonto?' Something he knew about.

Mr Noble was not liked and never would be.

'Does it hurt?' Norman asked as the lunch bell went.

'It bloody stings. Look at my hand. Stupid, bloody History.'

The next day the two of them hung back when the bell rang. They sneaked into the History classroom, opened the lid on the teacher's desk and Vince stuffed the strap up his jersey. On the way downtown they made the turning into the railway station. Vince reached under his jersey. He threw the strap on to the coal tender of the train which was standing at the platform. By the time they had returned to school, the strap was well on its way to Edinburgh. They had used up all of the lunch break but it had been worth it. 'Stupid, bloody History,' he said again.

Mr Noble was furious. For the rest of the week he quizzed all who passed through his classroom, paying particular attention to those who had recently been strapped. Little did he realise that the object in question had long since left the area. 'If I find out who was responsible for stealing my strap, I will punish them severely. Do you know who the culprit is?' he asked

Vince for the second time.

'No, sir,' was the reply.

Of all the school teachers Mr Noble was the least liked. He was six feet tall, had grey, thinning hair and a beaked nose. His snout reminded Vince of the puppet head that he had made out of papier-mâché at Berrydale Junior, except that Vince reasoned that the puppet was far more handsome. Vince's contempt for the man was growing weekly. Noble had little patience with Norman and his disability. Vince had swapped his desk with another lad just to be close to his chum. The two of them had developed a system whereby Vince would write in larger letters to enable Norman to look over the notepaper on Vince's desk, making it slightly easier for Norman to get through the period. This system did not prove infallible but it did help in reducing the wrath of the beak-nosed teacher. Norman was also on the receiving end of the black, leather strap on more than one occasion, as were most of the others in the class. The first time Norman was strapped, Vince had been unable to control his emotions and had uttered some remark which the teacher had overheard. It resulted in six of the best for Vince as well. On the bus home that afternoon, Vince could be heard by all as he vented his feelings.

'I'm gonna tear his fuckin' face off and put it in an envelope and post it to his house, the beak-nosed, fuckin' arse!'

'Calm down, Odd Job,' Norman said. 'I haven't been strapped any more than the rest of you, although you seem to be going for a world record.' Vince would not calm down. The others gave him a wide berth for the time being. They could hear him muttering for quite some time.

'Stupid, bloody History. Bugger the French Revolution. Beak-nosed, fuckin' arse!'

*

Vince arranged to meet Alex at the bus stop in town. They were going to the pictures. The Beatles film *Help* was playing that week. The bus journey took half an hour.

'Hello, have you been waiting long?'

'No, I've just got here.' She was wearing a short skirt and long boots. Her long, blonde hair was newly washed. Her green eyes sparkled and her smile showed off her perfect teeth. They walked the short distance to the picture house and settled in the back balcony just as the lights went down. The balcony was a little more expensive than the stalls but it was the place to be with your girlfriend. The coming attractions were over with and the main feature started to roll. They had both been looking forward to this one. It was in colour. Vince put his arm around Alex and she snuggled close with a dreamy look in her eyes. Their neighbours in the surrounding seats were already down to business when Vince kissed Alex on the cheek. She turned and offered her lips. Vince was keeping one eye on the couple who were further along in the seating. They seemed to be at a more advanced stage than the two novices. 'Maybe you're supposed to get straight to it,' thought Vince. The fellow was having a rummage about in the girl's blouse with no resistance being shown. 'I'll have to do something,' he thought. 'It'll be expected of me.' Alex was giving his mouth a good inspection with her tongue when he started on her buttons. He sneaked a hand down her front but didn't quite get to where he wanted to be. He chanced another button. This time he was able to reach the plateau of her firm breasts. His heart was thumping as he went for the third button but she stopped him.

'No, please don't.' Alex wanted to say *yes* but she was scared as well as excited. 'Let's watch the film.'

The two lovebirds had difficulty concentrating on the film. Someone was looking for a sacred ring that Ringo had. They cuddled a little later on with Vince approaching from the south this time, starting from her knee, but to no avail. The film finished and they all stood up for *The Queen.*

'You want to go to the chipper?' he asked.

'I'm not hungry, what about you?'

'No, neither am I,' he said as they walked hand in hand, looking in the shop windows.

'What time's your bus?' she asked.

'I can get the last one if you like? I've plenty of time.'

'We can go back to my house and listen to the radio. Mum and Dad are out and won't be back till late.'

'OK,' they stopped to kiss again.

Alex lived in a nice street near the centre of town and it was very handy for the shops and buses. It wasn't long before they arrived at her front door. The houses were made up of four flats with Alex and her parents living on the first floor. She switched on the living room light and went through to her bedroom to where her radio was already tuned to Radio Luxembourg. She turned it on and they both settled on top of her bed. They lay listening to Gerry and the Pacemakers singing *I Like It*. When

Elvis came on they moved closer. In the dark room, he could feel her breath on his cheek. They started kissing again. Her heart was thumping as her breasts pressed into his body. His hand moved up her legs to her thighs and she offered little resistance as he felt her womanhood through her pants. She was flushed and breathing heavily now. 'Stop, stop! Please.' She wasn't ready to join the other girls at school who had already done it. They carried on kissing and this time he was allowed to undo all of the buttons on her blouse. He ventured further but was stopped again. He was confused. 'Maybe I should wait until Cliff comes on the radio and see if I have more luck with him.' He knew that Cliff was one of Alex's favourites. 'What's wrong?' he asked, trying to get his breathing back to normal. 'Nothing,' she whispered. 'Just give me more time.' They kissed, cuddled and breathed heavily while listening to the sounds of the sixties in the background, stopping only long enough for refreshments with the occasional visits to the kitchen to get themselves a Coke and orange juice. Vince had to run to catch the last bus. They had lost all sense of time. He was still hot and sweaty when he reached his house. His Dad was sitting in front of the TV with a glass of beer in his hand.

'Enjoy the pictures, Vince?' Matthew asked.

'Yes, Dad it was fine.'

'What did you see?'

'The new Beatles film.'

'Did you go with Spike?'

'Naw, just someone from school, you wouldn't know them.'

Matthew grinned. 'Oh to be young again,' he thought.

'Is there any jobs I can help with, Dad? I could use some extra pocket money.' Vince was thinking about the overheads that he was starting to accumulate with the responsibility of having a girlfriend.

'Oh, I suppose I could find you something to do.'

'I'll do anything.'

'Are you doing alright at school? Can we expect good reports next time round?'

'Eh...I'm doing much the same as everyone else...I think,' Vince replied, laying the foundation for what he knew was likely to be an unfavourable school report when the teachers got around to writing it at the end of term. He wasn't learning much about the school curriculum. He had more important things on his mind. Maybe he'd have more luck with Cliff next time. Vince went to bed that night but he didn't sleep very well. In town, a teenage girl with long blonde hair was having a similar problem. It was a week later that they became members of *The Stupid Grin Club*. They had been larking about in the wood when their love was consummated. Vince met Alex that day at the bus stop in Berrydale. He had been teaching her how to ride his bicycle. The two of them had been running and chasing one another when their adult hormones had taken them both by surprise. It was over and done with very quickly, leaving them both slightly confused as to what all the fuss was about. They would have to get more practice at every opportunity if they were to get it right. Cliff was nowhere to be seen.

*

'Look out! Here comes Stumpy!' The girls were having a sneaky puff at the far side of the playground when the janitor appeared. He was heading over to where the girls were standing in a cloud of smoke. Lucy had produced a ten packet of cigarettes and she, Alex and Wendy were puffing away whilst trying to catch up with the gossip. This was Wendy's first attempt at having a smoke, the others were veterans. The girls were comparing notes about boys with most of the questions being fired at Alex. She had brought a different look about her to school that day after her woodland experience with Vince. Alex had tried to avoid talking about her admission into the adult world, but joining *The Stupid Grin Club* was like having a giant beacon stuck on top of your head. A lot of the new members tried to be casual about joining this elite club but no matter how good an actor you were, you just could not fool anyone, particularly if they were your close friends.

'Well, go on. Tell us what happened.'

'Eh, you know, it just happened.' Alex blushed as she replied to Lucy's question. 'It didn't last very long. Was it the same for you?'

'Yeah,' Lucy replied. Wendy was listening intently to see if she could pick up some tips. She was the only one of the three still waiting to become a member and was concerned that this might affect her relationship with her chums. She knew that Lucy had done it some time ago. That had been discussed in great detail. She had been with one of the school prefects and he had boasted about it to the whole school. She was getting the looks and being called a slag. Lucy promised herself that she would be fussier in future. Wendy had been fairly comfortable with her virginity up until then. She had been keeping up quite nicely with the rest of them, having had her periods start just after Lucy but some time before Alex. Now she was slipping down the ladder again. 'Christ,' she thought, 'the pressure, and me the minister's daughter as well.'

The girls at school were gradually falling like ninepins. Wendy had assumed that she would join this club soon, somewhere along the way. Alex was not forthcoming with any more details. They had moved on to another topic when Stumpy reached them. The janitor had made his way to where the plume of smoke was. He knew that this was another group of pupils trying out the dreaded weed. It didn't matter to him whether they smoked or not, after all, he enjoyed a puff himself. But, rules were rules and he had to be seen to do his duties. Hendry enjoyed his job at the school. He had been there as janitor since returning from the war all those years before. He'd lost his left leg just below the knee, during a desert skirmish in the last few weeks of fighting. The land mine had killed two of his regiment and injured even more. He considered himself one of the lucky ones and was shipped home to Blighty soon after. He had been fitted with an artificial limb soon after leaving the military hospital and when the job as school janitor had become vacant he had grabbed it with both hands and a leg. Hendry even had a house paid for by the school and lived opposite the main gate. He considered himself an integral part of the education system as he went about his business, doing his rounds.

'Now then girls, you know you're not supposed to be smoking in the playground. Put the cigarettes away. You'll be getting me into trouble with Mr Lattimer. I'm supposed to confiscate them you know, so just put them away. Wait till you're outside the gates.'

'You want a puff?' asked Alex, knowing that the janitor was on their side.

'No, not just now, girls, go on, put them away.'

'OK Hendry. Thanks.' They put the stubs back in the packet with Wendy's being the longest. She didn't think she'd ever get the taste for them no matter how many she tried. Wendy would have a few more attempts over the coming months but eventually she would give the habit a miss. The bell rang and the three of them headed off their separate ways for the next class, still chatting about that wonderful invention called boys. Wendy took consolation in having her bra strap pinged as she filed into the English class. 'I'll have to have a look in the mirror tonight,' she thought as she made her way to her desk. 'I'm sure they've grown since yesterday.'

*

They were fast approaching the end of their years of education. It had been interesting to say the least. The thoughts of all were on finding a job, apart from Lucy who was staying on another year and then going to college. Vince had the option of working with the council. His Dad could get him a job working with him. Wendy wanted to be a nurse. Everyone thought that she would make a good nurse because of her caring nature. Harry was to serve his time as an apprentice joiner. He had already spoken to the builder over on the other side of town and it was decided that he would start immediately he left school. Podger had his eye on a job in the music industry or at least working in the instrument shop of Simpson Reid. He could bash away at the drums

whenever he liked. Norman would end up working with the local paper, *The Spokesman*. He would start at the bottom sweeping floors, making tea and running errands.
This would suit him fine. Dealing with the public with his hearing problem was not a comfortable thought. He would feel far better in a close, working environment. As for Spike, he couldn't care less. If a job came along, then fine.

The penultimate day at school was to be taken up with prize-giving. Not that it made any difference to the raggedy-arsed bunch from Berrydale. They had no chance of coming out of the system with anything other than a better understanding of the University of Life and a piece of paper that would serve as an alibi for the last three years. The certificate would be shown to the disappointed parents who would have been more than delighted with the odd Higher here and there and not the blank slate that was being offered up by their offspring. Norman did achieve something. It was a wooden carved plaque that was presented by Mr Munro to Norman for being such an artistic scholar in the Woodwork class. It was to find a home beside the cake-stand that held the coats. There was also a special presentation made to the most popular pupil who had attended the academy. This girl or boy would be chosen by the teaching staff. It was not even worthy of a discussion by the Berrydale gang. They knew they were never likely to be nominees. Lucy would have won a prize had there been one for being the biggest tease. With the award ceremony over, they were now looking forward to the last day. They were promised a day out at the seaside, travelling there by bus. Unfortunately, the teachers would be there, but when it was announced that there was a challenge football match organised between the pupils and the staff, everyone started to look forward to it.

The big day arrived and they all piled into the bus. The teaching staff looked strangely out of place in their casual clothes. They had shed the old fashioned suits and dresses in favour of a more relaxed look. It still did not work for some of them. Mr Noble was wearing a pair of white shorts and white tennis shoes. On his head was a white trilby hat. The Berrydale gang thought it made him look like the Bald Headed Eagle seen in some of the cowboy movies or maybe a totem pole. They concluded that if Tonto had been around that day, he would have felt quite at home. Mrs Goddard also wore white shorts, much different from the skirts they were used to seeing her wear. This was the first opportunity the pupils had to view her splendid legs without having to resort to acrobatic feats. The journey to the seaside took forty minutes, much to the relief of the teaching staff. They were glad to get off the bus and away from the barrage of abuse directed at them. Mr Lattimer was trying to organise the pupils into teams of ten to make them more controllable but it was a losing battle. He had taken along the hoops of coloured bands that were used to distinguish the different teams on sports day. They were already being used as slings, bandages and head bands in a mock battle that had started on the bus between two teams of pirates. The affray spilled out of the coach and on to the grass, assaulting each other with mock swords and invisible cannons and causing the usually unflappable Mr Lattimer to lose his cool. He managed to get some semblance of order restored for the pending football match. The first game was to be five of the teaching staff versus the same number of pupils, with Mrs Goddard making up the numbers on the teachers' side. Podger and Vince were delighted to be chosen for the first team out. The jackets were placed down on the grass as makeshift goalposts and the whistle was blown by Mr Lattimer, the referee. The rest of the bus party lined up to cheer on their heroes. Vince and Podger decided to play up front as strikers, not that it made much difference to the shape of the team. They were just determined to be there to get the better of the teachers. The first goal was scored very quickly by Podger who headed in a cross from Vince. The teachers responded with two goals before the whistle went for half-time. Mr Munro had slotted in the equaliser. The Bald Headed Eagle had scored the second one to give the teachers a two one advantage. He barged his way through, knocking Podger and another team member over and sank the ball in the goal. Plan B was put into place. This involved a sneaky manoeuvre with one of the jackets, while play was down at the other end. Vince would have levelled the game soon after had he not been hacked down by Mr Noble just as he was about to score.

'Penalty ref!' the crowd shouted. The referee shook his head and waved play on.

'Oh, come on ref, for God's sake!' It did not make any difference to the decision. By the time Vince had picked himself up off the ground, Mr Noble had scored again, despite the moving of the goalpost jacket.

'Right, plan C!' Vince shouted to Spike who was

chatting to one of the girls in the crowd. Spike had another sort of game in mind.

'Spike, you arse!' Spike nodded in acknowledgement but carried on talking to his new found challenge.

The losing team was now three one down with about ten minutes left to play and it was with a fresh determination that they charged at the opponents. Vince had the ball and was going to make sure that it ended up in one place only. Podger was running with him, heading for Mr Noble who was standing in Podger's path waiting with a grin on his face. Podger ran full smack into him just as the History teacher was about to tackle Vince. The ball sailed in between the jackets and past Mrs Goddard who had been in goal. The game was levelled three minutes later by a similar movement. This time it was Vince's turn to whack the teacher, making sure that his knee caught Noble between his legs. Mr Noble was on the ground, groaning loudly and complaining to the referee about foul tactics. Mr Lattimer, who wasn't fit enough to keep up with play, had just arrived from the other end and did not witness the assault on one of his staff. The winning goal came just before the final whistle. Mr Noble, The Bald Headed Eagle, was limping badly and wasn't able to keep up with play as Vince slotted home the winner. The losers were at a distinct disadvantage anyhow. They had not seen the extra player. Spike had been on the pitch for the last five minutes. The teachers were so engrossed in the game that they hadn't noticed him helping out with the passing of the ball and the laughing crowd were not about to tell on him. Mrs Goddard saw Vince heading straight for her and she ran out of goal and tried to stop him. Vince quickly flicked the ball past her to score the winner. He couldn't stop himself as he ran into her, knocking her over. He bounced off her just as the two of them went down with Vince's head resting between her legs.

'Isn't this bloody game wonderful,' he thought, admiring the view. 'Are you alright Mrs Goddard?' he mumbled, his mouth full of white shorts.

'Eh...yes...Vincent. Can you, eh...let me up, please?' The two of them rose to their feet. It was difficult to tell who had the biggest grin as the final whistle went. The crowd cheered madly as their heroes walked off the pitch. Vince walked past the History teacher who was sitting down, clutching his stomach.

'You cheated, Wright,' he spat.

The striker laughed and murmured, 'Stupid fuckin' arse.'

Alex was standing with Lucy and Wendy, cheering on the lads. They had been waiting for two of the prefects to assemble the net for volleyball. Further along the playing field, the game was ready to start. The area had been marked out with the coloured bands salvaged from the pirate fight. The girls were being led off by Mrs Goddard. She would supervise the volleyball and leave the football to the male teachers. They would have to manage without her. Vince crept up behind Alex and grabbed her arm. 'Come on, Alex.'

'Where are we going?' she giggled. 'Mrs Goddard will notice.'

'Who cares, it's the last day, isn't it? We'll sneak away.' They waited for the right moment and ran behind a nearby sand dune. Vince had to have his kissing lesson before they went any further.

'Where are we going, Odd Job?' she sighed.

'Let's go and look for shells and crabs and sea monsters.'

'Oh yeah, we'll get all wet.' They ran down to the water to start exploring, stopping only for a brief moment to enjoy some more kisses. They removed their shoes and socks and waded into the sea water until the waves were lapping the tops of their shorts. They rolled them up as far as they could to prevent the water reaching their backsides. They needn't have bothered. A few moments later they were completely soaked. A wave had swept them off their feet toppling them into the salty water.

'Odd Job!' Alex screeched as she clung to his shirt.

'It's alright, Alex, I've got a hold of you,' he laughed. They were sitting down with their heads above the surface.

'It's bloody freezing!' she uttered, spitting out the salty water.

'It's not that cold. We could learn to swim. Hold on to my neck and put your legs out.' Alex did as she was told and was gracefully moving her legs when she let out another shriek.

'What is it now?'

'There's something in the water. Let me up! It's a creepy crawly!'

'Of course there's something in the water, there's lots of things swimming around, maybe it's a sea monster come to get us.'

'Odd Job, please let's get out of here, I'm scared!'

Alex was clinging on to Vince, her long, blonde hair dripping wet on his shoulder. They waded back to shore and fell down laughing. 'We'll have to get our clothes dry,' said Vince, taking off his shirt and shorts.

'I'm not taking anything off, someone will see me.'

'And how are you going to get dry, Alex? Don't be shy.'

'Well, OK, but only my blouse and shorts. You did this on purpose, didn't you?'

'Oh, come on Alex. Stop being such a prude.' She stripped off to her bra and pants. Vince had a huge smile on his face. 'Alex has such a beautiful body,' he thought.

'It's a bit cold.' She shivered, moving closer for a cuddle.

'Shall we go back in the water or should we get some practice?' He ran his fingers through her wet hair.

'Odd Job, is that all you think about? Let's go back in,' she giggled. 'What about that creepy crawly thing? Will it bite me?'

'If it doesn't, I will.' He chased her down to the water's edge, pausing briefly to throw their clothes over a large rock to dry in the sunshine. Vince jumped in with a splash causing Alex to topple over and get wet again. She grabbed some seaweed and threw it over his head, making him look like the monster from the deep lagoon. They went looking for crabs, turning over rocks to see what weird and wonderful things they could find, and when they were fed up doing that, they started making sand castles using a piece of wood as a makeshift shovel. They were so engrossed in what they were doing that they didn't notice the line of pupils and teachers watching from the distance.

'Alexandria! Vincent! What do you think you are doing?' It was Mrs Goddard. 'Come out of there at once!' shouted the angry teacher.

'Aw, bugger off, we're finished with school,' Alex heard herself reply.

'Well, really!' The teacher turned away and stomped back to the field.

'That's my woman,' thought Vince. 'That's my woman.'

Alex and Vince rejoined the rest to the thunderous applause from their school mates. The beach bums had been oblivious to the time of day. They had missed the rest of the sports and the picnic. Mrs Goddard had wanted to say something to get her point across but thought better of it considering it was the last day of school. She didn't want to chance losing face in front of the others. After all, it was meant to be a fun day out.

'You missed all the games, Odd Job,' said Harry.

'You think so,' grinned Vince. 'I don't suppose you've saved anything for us to eat, have you?'

'We've kept some sandwiches for you.' Wendy handed over the food that was wrapped in tin foil. 'There's a couple each for you, it's corned beef. There wasn't much choice.'

'Thanks, Wendy, you're a doll. What time does the bus leave? Does anybody know?'

'Christ knows,' said Spike, arriving at the scene with the others to catch up with the gossip. 'What have you two buggers been doing? Alex, your hair's all wet. Has Odd Job been washing it for you?'

'We've had a great day. We had no idea it was so late. Did anything interesting happen at the sports?'

'No, Mr Noble seems to have lost his enthusiasm.'

'What about you girls? Was the volleyball to your liking?' asked Vince.

'It was pretty boring, really. We should have been at the beach with you and Alex. Was the water warm?'

'It was OK once we were in. We didn't notice that much. There's plenty of creepy crawlies, isn't there, Alex?' Vince was pulling a funny face, trying to torment her.

'Stop it, Odd Job, or I'll throw you back in the sea.'

'The buses are here!' someone shouted.

'Come on, let's see if we can annoy the teachers again.'

They boarded the vehicles that would transport them back, jostling for prime seating. They were to be dropped off at the nearest point to where they stayed. All the Berrydale gang, apart from Spike, were in the same bus. He had decided to go in the coach going back to town. He'd been captivated by the smile of a girl and after a brief chat they had decided to go to the café for a Coke.

The teachers who were in charge of the travel arrangements didn't seem to care much by now as each bus filled up. They casually glanced around, trying to show some interest but it was obvious by their faces that they'd had enough. They just wanted to go home to get away from this riff-raff. Vince and Alex had parted company. She was on one of the buses that was going directly into town. The pirate fight started again, the noise drowning out any possibility of hearing the sing-song that

Mr Lattimer was attempting to start. The pupils were not interested in silly songs when there was business on the high seas to attend to. The paper plates and cups left over from the picnic were being used as cannon balls and the broadsides were aimed at the teaching staff. They were glad when the bus reached the village of Berrydale. Once more the affray spilled out as the bus stopped at the post office. The few people who were out and about in the village were quite amused at the drama that was taking place in their village centre. The back window of the bus was open and the fight was in full swing with every available object being used for the battle. A football had been chucked out of the window and was now being kicked against the bus. Podger aimed a ferocious kick at the open window and missed. The ball swerved and hit the post office window with a resounding crash, bringing the pirate fight to an end. The pupils in the fighting scattered and went their separate ways, leaving Mr Lattimer the task of writing to the post office to apologise for the breakage and request the return of the school football. The gang were now singing, 'No more school for us, no more shitey bus.'

Chapter Seven
1968. Podger starts Work.

It was a Monday when Podger stood at the door of Simpson Reid, wearing a new suit, shirt and tie. He had caught the eight o'clock bus into town and was ten minutes early for opening time. He pressed his face against the window and could see the object of his desire on show: a gleaming new Ludwig drum kit. He rubbed his hands together and thought, 'You're all mine.'

'Hello, lad, you're on time.'

'Yes, Mr Simpson.' He hadn't noticed the boss arrive.

'Are you eager to make a start, then?'

'Yes, Mr Simpson.'

'Right, first things first, I'll show you where we make the tea. How about a cuppa?'

'No, I'm fine, thanks.'

'No, lad, I meant how about a cuppa, there's the kettle, you make it!'

'Yes, Mr Simpson.'

'From now on you are the junior. You make the tea, understand?'

'Yes, Mr Simpson. When do I start to sell the instruments?'

'You'll start by helping Molly with the records. We'll see how you get on with that then we can have a chat, OK?'

'Yes, Mr Simpson.'

Molly arrived, hung up her coat and was already behind the record counter.

'Molly, here's your new assistant. His name is Robert. You can show him the ropes.'

'OK, Mr Simpson, I'll look after him.'

'So, it's Robert, is it?' She looked at the young man before her. He was average height, overweight, with wavy brown hair, blue eyes and, on his face, the remains of some freckles. The suit that he was wearing was on the small side but she figured that was the nearest size the shop would have had.

'Well actually, most people call me Podger, but Robert is fine.'

'Don't mind Simpson. He's a bit of a grump, just keep out of his way. He knows shite all about anything but he is the boss. His father started the business with Mr Reid. They're both retired now so Simpson Junior is in charge. He came straight from college with some degree or another. He probably studied on how to be an arse.'

Podger was starting to like his new workmate. She had a mischievous look about her. They would get on fine. He spent the rest of the day unpacking records to put on the shelves with the occasional trip to visit the kettle at teatime. Podger had an hour for lunch so he popped in to Antonio's to see Susan and her sticky buns.

'Hello, Podge, you alone then?'

'Yeah, I started work today at Simpson Reid. I'm on

my lunch hour.'

'What are you doing there? Shop assistant?'

'I thought I would be selling the instruments but I'm on the records, in between making the bloody tea.'

'You'll be working with Molly then. She'll keep you right. I'll have to pop in and see you, I want to get that new Beatles record.'

Two mugs of tea and three sticky buns later he was back in the shop. He made straight for the Ludwig kit and sat on the stool to see how it felt.

'What are you doing, lad? Get back to the records, now.'

'Yes, Mr Simpson.'

He was ready to leave at five o'clock along with Molly when Simpson caught up with him at the door.

'Where are you going, lad?'

'Home, it's five o'clock.'

'Not yet, lad. You haven't swept the floor or dusted the counter. That's part of your job you know.'

'Yes, Mr Simpson.'

'I'll give you a hand, Robert. You'll know to do it tomorrow, quarter of an hour before closing time.'

'Thanks, Molly.' The two of them swept the floor, emptied the ashtrays and wiped the counter down.

'Can we go now, Molly?'

'Yeah. We're finished, come on.'

'Goodnight, Molly, goodnight, lad,' he shouted from his office.

'Goodnight, Mr Simpson,' they both replied.

'Fuck you, Mr Simpson,' Podger added, under his breath.

'Are we ever going back to Ferguson's?' asked Norman.

'Have you any suggestions? We've looked everywhere apart from the house,' said Vince. 'I can't think.' They had spoken about the gold coins many times. Three years had passed since they'd helped clean the building and they were at a loss as to what to do. It hadn't helped that Julie and Sebastian had never come back.

'Are we going to do anything? We've to start work next week.'

'Yeah, yeah, yeah, I know. Let's have another look on Friday when he's at the Mart. There must be something that we missed.'

'Wonder how Harry and Podge are getting on. They'll be home about six, won't they?'

'Has Spike got anything lined up yet?' Vince asked.

'No, I shouldn't think so. He'll probably be at home watching TV, the lazy bugger.'

'What do you suppose she looks like now?'

'What! You just saw him the other day.'

'No, Norman. She! I said, not He!' said Vince, raising his voice.

'Who?'

'Julie. I was just wondering what she looks like. Now she'll be grown up.'

'She looked pretty grown up before. Do you think her boobs are even bigger now?'

'We need to meet some girls. We could go to the dance at Burnside on Saturday.'

'How can we, have you got any money?'

'I'll try Mum again. She wants me to hurry up and

start getting a wage so I can pay something for my keep. What about you?'

'Yeah, I'm the same. I'll probably be working for nothing for a year, paying back the money that I owe my Dad.'

'It's nearly six, let's go and meet the bus.'

The two workers came off the bus, Podger looking splendid in his suit, Harry looking dirty in his overalls.

'Christ, Podge! You're a smart bugger. Well, how was it?'

'Pretty boring, that Mr Simpson, he's an arse.'

'Did you get a bash on the drums?'

'Not yet, but I will.'

'I had a boring day as well. Me and Podge were just saying on the bus that we've become experts at making tea.'

'Speaking of tea, I'm starving.'

'Didn't you get anything to eat, Podge?'

'I went in past Antonio's.'

'Oh, and did you see the lovely Susan?'

'Yup, I think she's got the hots for me.'

'Some chance.'

'Are you non-workers going to the dance on Saturday?'

'We'd like to, but we're a bit short on cash.'

'You want a sub? We'll have a wage packet by then.'

'Great, that saves asking at home.'

'It's only a sub, we need it back. Are you both paid by the week when you start work?'

'Yeah, next week.'

'That's settled then. We can meet up. We'll get

somebody to go into the Burnside Arms to buy a half bottle.'

'We're in the money, we're in the money.'

'Harry, for goodness sake, look at the state of you, you're covered in shite. You're beginning to look like Patrick.'

'So what, I was working, not like you two layabouts. I had to sweep up plaster and stuff. It gets right up your nose and look at the state of my hair. It's white. I'm going to need a bath every day by the look of things. I think I picked the wrong trade.'

'It's money, isn't it? Stop grumbling.'

'Yeah, I suppose.'

'What's on TV tonight?'

'Dunno. Did you see *The Avengers* the other night? I fancy that Diana Rigg.'

'Well, I'm off for my tea,' said Harry.

'There goes that bloody word again. Tea, tea, make the tea, lad. Yes, boss, here's your bloody tea. Hope you choke on it.'

*

Norman and Vince cycled to the big tree. They were perched on a branch overlooking Ferguson's place, patiently waiting for him to go off on his weekly visit to the Mart. They'd been there for an hour and were thinking that they must have picked the week that he'd decided to stay at home when he drove off in his Land Rover, heading in the right direction. They gave him ten minutes to make sure that he was well on his way, before jumping on their bikes and cycling down to the farm. The caravan was still there. The glossy exterior had faded a bit now.

They tried the door but it was locked.

'Let's have another look in the court.'

They went slowly through the barn, checking everything that they had checked before. There were a lot more sacks this time and some turnips left over from winter. They went up the stair to where the barley was kept and past the swallow's nest.

'You know that the swallows go all the way to Africa at the end of summer and then turn around and come back again. That's pretty clever, don't you think?'

'Yup, Norman, that's clever. These walls are solid aren't they?'

'Yes, and the floors.'

'Well, there's nothing that could possibly be hidden in here. Is there?'

'No. Bloody hell! That smell of shite is still horrible.'

They went back outside and over to the shed that they'd cleaned all those years before. The door had a louder creak to it now as they pushed it open.

'Look at the stuff he has in here now. It's worse than ever.' They sat down on top of one of the chests and had a good look round.

'Look, there's my drawing of Julie's boobies, beside the four-leafed clover.'

'I've told you, Odd Job. It's a shamrock.'

'I know, I know, I was only joking.' They sat and pondered for half an hour and came to the conclusion that they would never find the bloody, gold coins.

'Aw, come on, let's go home.'

*

The Burnside Arms was situated at the town limit. A

bus ride and a short walk got them there. The pub had a large room at the back which served as a dance hall. It was proving to be a popular place at the weekends. There were always plenty of bands wanting to play there. This weekend it was the turn of Blackfoot, a four piece rock and roll band. Podger couldn't wait to offer his opinion on the drummer.

'He's not bad, could do better. Shite kit he has.'

'Well, sell him a better one. Get him a cup of tea at the same time.'

'Bugger off.'

They had apprehended an older bloke outside the pub door and had persuaded him to go in and buy them a half bottle of whisky. None of the bunch looked as if they would pass for eighteen, not even if they shaved as often as they could. The pub toilet had been chosen as the place where they would down the contents of the bottle. When it was his turn, Spike tried to drink the whole lot by himself. The empty bottle was thrown in the bin. The screwed up faces returned back to normal.

'Blimey, that's strong. Can we get a mixer next time?'

'We need another bottle. That one didn't last long and...Spike, you're last this time for a scoof.' Some fellow they knew wandered in to use the toilet so he was asked to go and get another bottle along with a bottle of a mixer. The raw whisky was still burning on the way down. He was handed the money after a quick whip-round and came back with the whisky and a bottle of Coke. Vince and Harry had a drink from the Coke bottle and then they poured in the Scotch. They had the bottle drunk dry in no time.

'Right, where's these girls?' asked Spike. The hall was busy by now and the band were in the middle of a Hollies number as the lads swaggered in to join the crowd. Vince noticed that Alex was there, dancing with a fellow.

'What's he doing with my bird?'

'Settle down, Odd Job, she's only dancing. Let's have a wander round.' The girls who were not dancing were sitting on the chairs at one side of the hall. The boys were sitting on the opposite side, having meaningful discussions with one another. 'Look at the tits on that!' Harry and Norman had plucked up courage to ask two girls sitting on their own to dance. The lads were soon doing a particularly fetching routine to *Twist and Shout*. Podger was wandering about looking for a less pretty one in the hope that he could get on the floor. He spotted one and turned to nudge Vince to get him to ask her friend but Vince had stopped to speak to Alex. She was standing half-way up the stairs that led to the bar.

'Hi, Alex, you here by yourself?' he asked, climbing up to her level.

'She's with me,' growled the fellow. 'Piss off!'

'I wasn't talking to you, mince head!'

Vince did not see the punch coming. All he knew was that he had joined the space programme for the second time in his life. He flew through the air at what seemed like an altitude of two feet and landed on a chap twice his size. 'Houston, we have a problem!' Vince thought. The big fellow took hold of Vince by his lapels, smiled in a funny sort of way and then stuck his head full force in the face of the astronaut. Alex rushed over and bent down, cradling his head. Her hankie was out and she was trying to stem the blood coming from his nose.

'Did I get the bugger?' Vince uttered to the vaguely familiar features that looked down at him.

'You've been drinking, haven't you?'

'I may have had a small one.' Vince was now on his feet and could just make out what was going on at the other end of the hall. His chums were getting a beating from the pals of the one who had butted Vince.

'Are we winning?'

'Odd Job, you're such an arse at times. That's why I like you so much and, no...you're not winning,' replied Alex. The fight had now stopped with the Berrydale lot licking their wounds.

'Does this mean you're still my bird? What about gormless features that you were with?'

'Of course, I'm your bird. He's not with me. We only just met.'

'Oh good, it hasn't been such a bad day after all then. I think I could just about manage a slow dance with your help. I'm a bit groggy.'

'Go and wash your face. You look like a boxer. Your nose is twice the size it should be,' she giggled.

'Oh, bugger, lots more for me to have to pick.'

'That was a bunch of no fun,' said a dishevelled Spike. 'Is that as sore as it looks?'

'You're no oil painting yourself, Spike. Come on you lot, let's get cleaned up. I want a last dance with Alex. Can we get an earlier bus home?'

'Does this mean you're off again? I'd see more of the Lone Ranger if he was my bloke.'

'Sorry, Alex, I'll see you in town, I start with my Dad

next week at the council. Besides, the Lone Ranger has got two black eyes, but he doesn't have a nose like mine.'
They snuggled closer. Vince had to breathe through his mouth.

'You stink of whisky. When are you going to grow up?'

'Never.'

A little later the boys were on the bus heading home. Vince had received his kissing lesson from Alex and had promised to look in past her work some lunchtime. She was to start working in the bowling alley that had just opened.

'Look at the state of our clothes. How do we explain this mess?'

'Blame them other blokes,' said Vince. 'Just say they started the fight. I could use a cup of tea Podge...Harry, did any of you bring the kettle?'

'Piss off!'

*

Vince had accepted his Dad's offer of a job. The two of them arrived at the council building on Monday morning. Matthew was an administrator in charge of the crew that did the outside work. He was responsible for maintaining the roadside in the summer and clearing the snow in winter. He was on a good wage by now, having been promoted from yard manager. He had already discussed with his son what his duties were to be. Vince was to start as a labourer helping the outside team. He was to avoid making the tea for the office staff. He had his very own flask and sandwiches tucked under his arm. The other workers nodded their greetings as they arrived for the day's work.

'What's wrong with his eyes?' he overheard someone ask. Vince had two black eyes as a result of his weekend fight. His nose was nearly back to normal. He was introduced to Wilf and Charlie, his work mates in the crew. They would be tidying the roadside in the town centre.

'Is that beside the new bowling alley?' Vince asked.

'Yez, why?' replied Wilf.

'No reason,' Vince answered, trying not to laugh at Wilf's speech impediment. His new work mate whistled through his teeth as he spoke. He sounded as if he was playing the recorder at the same time.

'Right, lez get going.'

They set off in the council van with Vince wedged between Charlie and Wilf. They spent most of the morning fixing kerbstones and Vince was glad when they stopped for lunch. His hands were blistered with the shovel he was using.

'We stop for an hour,' Charlie said. 'Sometimes we stretch it a bit over. I suppose we'll have to watch what we're doing now that we have the boss's son on the team. Is that right, lad?'

'I'm not a snitch. You don't have to worry about me.'

'Good lad.'

'Listen, I'm just going down the road to see someone. I won't be long.'

'Whez he off to, Charlie?'

'Dunno, he said he wouldn't be long.'

It took Vince five minutes to walk the short distance to the bowling alley. He found Alex behind the kiosk, handing over a pair of shoes to a customer.

'Hi there, this is a bit smart, isn't it?'

'Well well, it's my hero, the Lone Ranger, with a funny nose.' Vince didn't look unlike the masked man. Both his eyes were still visibly dark.

'Is Tonto with you?'

'Very funny. How's the job going?'

'Not bad, fancy trying the bowling sometime? What are you doing here anyway? I thought you started work today.'

'I have. I'm just up the road. I came in past to say hello.'

'You haven't got Silver with you? We're not allowed horses in here you know. How's your nose? Is it still sore?'

'It hurts like hell when I sneeze.'

'Serves you right. You're just a trouble maker. Do you want them girlie things that we use, to stick up your hooter?'

'What are you on about, Alex?'

'I heard about this woman that suffered from nose bleeds and she stuck, you know, up her nose to catch the bleeding.'

'She must have had a big nose. I think you're speaking nonsense.'

'Please yourself. I have to go. I'm getting funny looks from my supervisor. You'll have to get lost. Will we be meeting up at the weekend? I want to kiss your nose better.'

'Yeah, I'll be around somewhere. See you later.'

'Bye, and Odd Job, if your horse has shit in my lobby,

you'll have to clean it up yourself.'

'What happened to that shy girl I met in the playground?' he thought, grinning to himself. She was picking up all his bad habits. 'She'll be peeing with us men next!'

'Whez yez been?'

'I was speaking to my bird.'

'Whaz she like?'

'Bloody hooligan!'

*

Lucy bumped into Wendy at the bus stop in town.

'Hello, where have you been then?'

'I was at the hospital to find out when I can make a start. I go in on Monday, Ward Ten.'

'Great, do you think you'll like it?'

'I suppose so...What about you, how's school?'

'It's OK. I've a day off today, makes the weekend longer. I was looking round some shops.'

'Buy anything?'

'Only this top,' said Lucy, pulling it out of the bag.

'Oh, that's nice. Is it C & A?'

'Marks. I sometimes wish that I had a job like the rest of you. I'd like to have more money for clothes. My Mum and Dad have been good to me. Have you seen that new bowling alley that Alex works in?'

'No, what's it like?'

'It's huge. Do you fancy trying it?'

'I'd love to.'

'What about tomorrow, will your Dad let you?'

'I'm sure it'll be OK. I'll ask.' The bus arrived and the back seat was empty.

'We could challenge some of the lads,' continued Lucy. 'Let's go round and ask them this evening, but first we'll ask your Dad. I'll come with you.' They were at the Reverend's door half an hour later.

'Hello, Mr Calder.'

'Hello, Lucy. I haven't seen you for a while. How's school?'

'Fine, OK, just this term to do and then off to college. We were wondering if it's alright for Wendy to come with us to that new bowling alley in town?' Lucy smiled that special way that she'd been practising for some time now.

'Yes, well, I suppose so. You won't be back late, will you?'

'No, no, we're going to challenge some of the lads.'

'Oh, for goodness sake!'

'They're alright, Mr Calder, good for a laugh. So it's OK then?'

'Yes, yes, go ahead.'

On the day of the bowling there were four of them on the bus. They had asked around but only Podger and Harry could manage to accept the challenge from Lucy and Wendy. Spike wanted to watch the sport on TV and Vince and Norman had arranged something else. Alex was on duty. She had to work every other Saturday.

'Hello, you lot.'

'Hi, Alex, how's it going? We're in to try this bowling thing. Do we get a discount?'

'That'll be right. Everybody pays the same. You want me to get sacked? Where's that fellow with the big red nose and the two black eyes?'

'Why, do you fancy him?'

'No way, he looks dangerous. I'm a quiet, shy girl.'

'Yeah, we remember when you were. Odd Job is somewhere with Norman. Don't know where. What do we need for this bowling then?'

'Your shoe size first. Hurry up, Podge.'

'What?' He had his eye on the café that was selling the chips.

'Your shoes, take them off, preferably far away from me.'

'They're not half as bad as yours, Harry.'

'Shut up, you two, we're trying to listen to what Alex is saying about the scoring.' Lucy and Wendy had a rough idea of what to do. They had the piece of paper with the boxes on it.

'So that's a strike and that's a spare and...oh, come on you lot, let's get started.'

'Look, just fill in the boxes. I'll add it up when you've finished.'

'Thanks, Alex.' She put them on lane three. It was the nearest empty one and she could keep an eye on them from her kiosk.

'Gosh, that's heavy.' Wendy had picked up the nearest ball.

'There are lots of different weights and finger sizes. You'll just have to try them until you get one that fits,' said Alex.

'Give us the heavy ones,' said Harry, thinking that the heavier the ball the more chance of knocking all the pins down. 'You girlies have the lightest ones.' Harry picked up a bowling ball and aimed for the target. He had been watching the people in the next lane. A quick backwards swing and off the ball shot landing three feet in front of him with a thud. The ball veered to the right and landed in the gutter.

'Bugger, can I have that one back?'

'You can't have it back, stupid. That was your first shot. Podge will have to get the rest or less as a spare to score.'

'My turn,' said Podger, picking up the heaviest one. He was thinking along the same lines as Harry. His ball weaved its way towards the target and caught the three pins at the right hand side.

'You two are shite,' said Lucy. It was her turn now. She had been practising her backward swing while the lads were on. She wasn't going to make a fool of herself in front of all these people. She lined up, swung gracefully, released the ball and watched as it rolled straight for the centre pin. It only went off line at the last second, catching seven of the standing pins.

'Nice one,' said Wendy. 'Is it my turn now?' She had found a bowling ball with a snug fit and had been standing waiting her turn with the ball primed and ready to go.

'Take your time, Wendy. Aim for the three that are left.'

Wendy stood straight, feet together, aimed at the target, took three steps, a huge back swing and thrust forward. It looked very professional. The bowling ball was off down the lane at quite a nice speed, the only problem being she hadn't released the ball from her hand. Wendy landed flat on her stomach quite a few feet from the start line with her arm pointing south.

'Wendy, come back!' The three other bowlers were doubled up with laughter. 'You don't have to go with it.'

Wendy was lying in the lane with the ball still on line. It had wanted to go further but the drag factor had proved too much. Podger went to assist. 'Are you alright?' he asked, helping her on her feet. 'Give me the ball...let go of it.'

'I can't...it's stuck to my hand. Ouch! You'll have my fingers off. Stop!'

'Oops, it's stuck, right enough. Give us a hand someone.'

The others had a go at pulling the ball free but they seemed to be making matters worse. Alex was summoned to assess the situation.

'Stop struggling, that's not helping any. Your fingers will swell up and it will be more difficult to get free.'

'You'll never get that in the pocket of your jacket, Wendy.'

'Shut up, Harry.'

'Just tell everyone it's a bogey.'

'Shut up!'

'Sorry.'

'It's OK, Wendy, don't listen to him,' said Alex, putting a comforting arm round her. 'This has happened before. Come over to the kiosk. I have some butter. We'll soon get it off.'

'What if she has to sleep with it like that? She could turn over in the middle of the night and pull herself out of bed,' laughed Podger.

'Will you shut up. Can't you see that Wendy's upset?' said Alex. She was having a problem keeping a straight face herself.

It was a few minutes before they managed to get the bowling ball off Wendy's fingers, using the butter as a lubricant. She was persuaded to carry on with the game only after Alex had selected a ball with the correct size finger holes. 'Don't stand around holding on to the ball or your fingers will swell up in the holes,' Alex advised. The game was resumed with Wendy soon getting the hang of it. She managed two strikes and when Alex added up the scores at the end of the game, the girls were declared the winners.

'Well, you smart arses, what have you got to say for yourselves now?'

'Beginner's luck,' replied Podger, changing his shoes. 'Anyone fancy some chips?'

*

The sixties were the years of long hair, beads, love and peace and the Americans attending the Vietnamese war which was in full swing. The music was changing almost daily, as was the fashion. Spike had tried to enhance his sideburns with the help of some soot from the fireplace in an attempt to make himself look more interesting to the girls. It didn't work too well as he found out one night while he was having a smooch with his new found conquest. The poor girl ended up with a black face and Spike burst out laughing at the sight of it. She interpreted this outburst as him ridiculing her and she slapped his face before stomping off in a rage. She couldn't understand why she was being stared at on the way home on the bus. It was also around this time that Spike, much to the annoyance of his chums, developed a new language. He met up with Vince and Harry outside the post office after they had finished work.

'You got yourself a job yet, you lazy bugger?' asked Harry.

'No, man, I haven't got one yet, man.'

'Have you been looking for one?'

'Not really, man, Dad's asking me to help him at the Co-op with the lifting, man.'

'What, you've to help this lifting man? What's his name?'

'No, there isn't a lifting man, man. Dad wants a hand with the lifting, man.'

Vince was shaking his head. 'I think what Spike means, Harry, is that his Dad wants him to lend a hand with the lifting of the domestic appliances.' Spike was picking up a lot of Americanisms due to the number of TV programmes that he watched. He had a particular love of cartoons as well as the cops and robbers and cowboy movies that he digested. He knew all of Popeye's friends.

'Yeah, that's right, man. The lifting, man.'

'Can't you get a full time job at the Co-op? Your Dad will put in a word for you.'

'Yeah, he said he'd have a word with a man, man.'

'You've been watching too much television, Spike.'

'Yeah, peace and love. Do you know where I can get some beads, man?'

'Spike, you're a shite. You're going to have to get a job sometime, you know.'

'Yeah, I know, Harry, man.'

'What are you doing with that soot on your face? It isn't even the same colour as your hair, for God's sake.'

'Saw a picture of Elvis in a magazine. He's wearing his hair this style now, probably copied it off me.'

'Oh, I didn't know the King had a coal fire...sorry!'

'Yeah, well, word gets around. He probably has a couple in Graceland, man.'

'I'm off to get my supper. Some of us have been working, you know. I'll see you later.'

'Yeah, sure, man. See you later.'

They went their separate ways with Spike still muttering about peace and love. He would get a telling off from Donald, his Dad, for having that black mess on his face.

'You can help me tomorrow with the lifting, Ralph, and no excuses.'

'Sure, man, the lifting, man,' Spike muttered out of earshot as he went to switch on the TV. He never did acquire the beads for around his neck and he soon gave up on the soot enhancement on his sideburns. They would eventually grow the more that he shaved. This would be good preparation for the hairy-face era which would arrive sometime in the near future along with the bell-bottom trousers and the loud shirts. Spike would have to get a job to enable him to stay in the forefront of fashion. He wasn't about to be left behind whilst everyone else had that bit more flexibility with the wages they were earning.

'Bloody hell, it's tough being a young man, man,' he thought.

Chapter Eight
1969. Podger and the Dentist.

Podger woke up that morning with a nagging toothache. He tried to ignore it but was reminded at the breakfast table as he bit into a piece of toast and marmalade.

'What is it, Robert?' his Mum asked as he let out a squeal.

'It's my tooth...I've hardly slept. It's killing me.'

'You'd better phone the dentist. Let's have a look.' Podger opened his mouth and she could see that he had lost the filling on one of his lower teeth.

'That's your problem there,' she said, giving it a poke with her finger.

'Ouch, Mum! That hurts.'

'Take a couple of aspirins for now. I'm going to phone Mr Wilkins. Are you going to be alright for work?'

'I'll have to be...it's pay day. I'm off or I'll miss the bus.'

'Take this bottle with you. I've left you six. Don't take them unless you have to.'

Podger had difficulty trying to concentrate at the shop. Molly was very sympathetic. He tried to keep occupied to take his mind off the pain. Even making the tea was a way of keeping busy. By closing time he had swallowed all of the aspirins.

'You're very quiet today, lad,' said Simpson as he handed round the wages.

'Yes, Mr Simpson.' The journey home seemed to take ages and he was glad to walk through his front door.

'How is the tooth now, Robert?'

'It's murder, Mum. Have you phoned the dentist?' he asked, hoping she would say no. After all, the pain might be gone by next morning.

'You've an appointment tomorrow morning. They only take emergencies on a Saturday. I had to say that you were in extreme pain. Someone will have to go with you.'

'Aw, Mum, he won't give me gas, will he?'

'You can't go around with that constant pain. Maybe he'll manage to fill it. Do you want me or your Dad to go with you?'

Podger was starting to feel quite unwell by now. The thought of having to visit the butcher Wilkins was proving quite daunting. He had been there before and so had the others. It was not their favourite place to visit.

'Is it OK if I ask Spike or Odd Job to come with me?' He was on the lookout for spiritual help.

'Please yourself. Your appointment is for eleven o'clock.'

Podger tried to eat some supper. He'd had very little to eat that day. He scoffed down a few chips followed by some rice pudding before he wandered over to Vince's house. Spike was already there.

'Hi, Podge, you're looking a bit glum. Bad day at work?'

'I've got to go to the bloody dentist tomorrow. Any of you want to come along?'

'What time?'

'Eleven o'clock. Christ! I hate the dentist. He's a butcher.'

Spike and Vince agreed to meet Podger at the bus stop for the ten o'clock bus. Podger was yawning. He'd had another sleepless night.

'Is it still as bad? You won't want one of these sweets then?' asked Spike, handing round the bag of gobstoppers.

'No way!' was the reply, along with a faint rumbling of his stomach.

The back seat was full. They had to sit on separate seats. Podger elected to sit on his own. The other two sat together munching the sweets, much to his annoyance. He knew they were doing it on purpose.

The three of them were at the dentist's surgery by eleven. Vince and Spike sat either side of Podger in the reception area. Podger started to perspire and wanted to run away. He could hear the groans of a male victim coming from the closed door to his left.

'Don't worry, Podge. You're far braver than him. Sure you don't want a sweet?'

The door opened and a young lad came through with tears streaming down his face. Behind him was the dentist wearing a white coat with the odd spattering of blood down the front.

'I'm going home!' squealed Podger, rising half-way out of the chair.

'Robert Chalmers!'

'Go on, Podge, it'll soon be over. We'll wait for you,' said Spike, pushing him towards the door.

'Now then, young man, what seems to be the trouble?'

Podger felt like saying, 'It's my toenails, you stupid fool, can you cut them for me?' but instead he heard the words, 'My tooth is very painful, there's probably nothing much wrong with it.'

'Right, get in the chair, my boy and we'll have a look.'

Wilkins was a short, stout fellow, grey and balding with a moustache he played with when he spoke. He had a distinct waddle to his gait. He also had bad breath, Podger seemed to remember from his last visit. This was confirmed when he looked into Podger's mouth.

'Say ahh.'

'Ahh, ahh.'

'Uh huh, uh huh, I can see what the problem is. Rinse and spit.'

'Why don't you rinse and spit, yourself, you smelly bugger,' thought Podger.

'Well, my boy, I can't fill that,' said the dentist, twiddling his facial hair. 'That will have to come out. Have you brought someone with you to take you home?'

'Ye...ye...yes!'

'What's it to be then, needle or gas?'

'Eh...eh, I don't like gas and I don't like the needle,' whispered the voice from the chair.

'Well, we can't magic it out.' Podger could see that he was getting impatient.

'I don't want gas, I'll be sick. Actually, it feels much better now.'

'Right, the needle it is.' His assistant passed the

syringe to the master who jabbed it into Podger's gum.

'Ahh...*ahh!*' He could feel the cold liquid enter. He tried to close his mouth but the metal clamp prevented him from doing so. The dentist stuck the syringe in again from a different angle. His mouth was numb after the third injection. Podger tried to swallow but he couldn't muster the spit somehow. His hands were gripping the chair in fear.

'Oh Christ,' he thought, 'why have I got to go through with this?'

The girl assistant passed over some sort of stainless steel pliers and within seconds he could feel himself being pulled out of the chair. His head was yanked left then right and when it stopped, he sank into the seat.

'I'm glad that's over,' he thought, looking for the object that had caused him so much pain. Unfortunately the tooth was still attached to his mouth.

'Rinse and spit, my boy, this is a tough little devil.' The dentist continued with another stainless steel instrument that his assistant handed over. This one was used for leverage, trapping Podger's tongue in his teeth.

'*Ahh!*' The dentist stopped for a second to change back to the pliers. 'Sorry, son, was that your tongue? Keep it in.'

With a mighty yank the rotten tooth was out. Podger sank into the chair with a thud. He hadn't realised that his head could stretch so far from his body.

'Rinse and spit. Are you OK, boy?'

'Yesh,' was the reply as he brought the cup to his mouth and landed off target.

'Let me help you,' said the assistant, guiding it to his

lips for him.

'How do you feel?' she asked.

'Ash flee shine,' was the strange language being spoken from somewhere in the room.

'Here, take this,' she said, handing him a paper napkin.

'Shanks.'

Spike and Vince were reading the magazines when the door of the surgery opened and the zombie walked through. He looked strangely familiar to them. It looked like the fellow they had brought with them, except this one had staring eyes and his tongue didn't seem to fit in his mouth.

'Podge, are you alright?'

'Yesh, shanks.'

'What's wrong with your tongue?'

'Nusshen.'

The assistant who was holding on to him changed the red napkin for a white one, at the same time stuffing Podger's tongue back where it belonged. It didn't want to go back inside. She had to wedge it behind his lower teeth.

'Don't worry, the bleeding will soon stop and the numbness will go away by tomorrow. Just keep rinsing out, OK?'

'Yesh.'

'Come on, Podge.' Vince and Spike grabbed an arm each. 'Let's get you some fresh air.' The two of them walked the zombie down the stairs to the street.

'Are you OK?'

'Um deed a trink, um sirsty.'

'What's he saying?' Spike had let go of his arm and

was leaning on the wall doubled up laughing. It set Vince off and the pair of them started off in fits of laughter again. Podger opened his mouth to say something, hopefully in English, but the shot of cold air reminded him that he'd been at the dentist. 'Ahh!' he mumbled.

'Keep your mouth closed, you silly bugger. Come on, we'll go to Antonio's for something to drink.' They walked from the surgery to the café. It would have been easier to hop on a bus but they were trying to get their chum back to normal. In any case, he had to pause now and again to spit the blood from his mouth.

'What are we having?' Spike asked as they claimed the seat by the window.

'I'll have a Coke. What about you, Podge?'

'Shoringe tush.' That set the two of them off again. Susan came over to see what was so funny.

'Podge, what's wrong with your mouth? It's all lop-sided and your tongue's sticking out.'

'He's been to the dentist.'

'What, the butcher Wilkins?'

'The very same.'

'Oh Podge, you poor thing,' said Susan, giving him a hug. 'Is it sore?'

'Yesh, this is better,' Podger thought, snuggling into her hair.

'What are you having? You won't want a bun will you...maybe just something to drink?'

'Shoringe tush, slease.'

'What?' Susan was chuckling by now along with the other two who were sitting in the seat. She tried to keep a straight face but it was no contest.

'Get him a shoringe...I mean an orange juice, will you, Susan?'

Vince was still in fits along with Spike. Susan came back to the table with the drinks. 'There you are, Podge. I hope it makes you feel better.'

'Shanks.' He was very thirsty by now. He also wanted to get rid of the taste of blood. He eagerly grabbed the drink and hoisted it to his lips, tilting the glass to empty the contents. Not one drop managed to get through his battered mouth.

'Stop! For Christ's sake will you,' cried Spike, grabbing the glass out of his hand. The drink had run all the way down his chin and on to the table. Podger was trying with his redundant tongue to feel his way to the liquid. He was very thirsty and very angry.

'*Shuck, shuck, shuck!*' He offered in this new and strange language, banging his fist on the table. '*Shuck!*'

Vince and Spike were almost wetting themselves by now. Susan was behind the counter trying to give a customer change from the till. She could hardly see the keys because of the tears rolling down her cheeks. A couple who were sitting at another table were wondering why they were laughing at that poor, handicapped boy. 'They shouldn't be allowed out with the poor thing if they are going to behave like that.'

Susan had composed herself enough to fetch another glass with a straw this time. She guided the straw into his mouth careful not to stick it up his nose. With great relief Podger was at last able to quench his thirst. The others watched as the orange juice disappeared in double quick time.

'Snother, slease.'

'What?'

'Snother,' he said with frustration. '*Slease!*'

Susan came back with the third glass which was dispatched just as quickly followed by a loud burp.

'Feeling better, now?'

'Yesh.'

Podger was just cleaning himself up with a towel Susan had brought, when the feeling came over him. 'Um sheeling shick.'

They pulled him through to the toilet just in time for him to throw up in the urinal. There was too much fluid to go through his frozen mouth. The bulk of it had to find another passage way. It squirted out of his nose like the water from a garden hose, a mixture of blood and orange juice. He was very angry by now. '*Aw shor shuck shake!*'

Further cleaning up had to be done on this sorry sight before they returned to their seats. The couple at the other table had left shaking their heads in disbelief. 'Someone should do something. It's a disgrace!'

Spike and Vince managed to get Podger to the bus stop without further incident apart from a brief stop for a spit. Podger still could not feel much around the mouth area although he had a little more control of his tongue.

'Are you alright, Podge, you're not feeling shick again, are you?'

Spike had to sit down on the pavement. He couldn't stand for laughing.

'The bus should be along any minute now,' said Vince.

'Snot sunny.' Podge was still in a rage.

'No, it's not, you're right. It's all this rain we're having. Maybe the sun will come out later.'

'*Shuck shoe suggers!*'

The bus arrived and they had no sooner sat down in the back seat when Podger fell fast asleep.

'He looked like a snake there for a while with his tongue hanging out,' remarked Spike to Vince. That was all that was needed to start another fit of the giggles. The other commuters turned to see what the commotion at the back was.

'Oh, it's only them lads from Berrydale,' someone said. 'They'll be up to no good again.'

'Wake up, we're here. Come on, wake up, Podge.'

The bus had to wait for a few minutes while they roused him from his sleep. He had a terrible taste in his mouth, much worse than before.

'Um sirsty!'

'You'll be home in a minute. You'll get a drink there. Has your mum got shoringe tush?'

They walked the sleeping beauty off the bus and up to his front door.

'Hello, Mr Chalmers.'

'Hello, lads. Robert, are you OK?'

'He'll be fine. He had to have the tooth out. The dentist froze his mouth. He should be OK in the morning. He's very sirsty...I mean thirsty. He fell asleep on the bus as well. We'll see you later. Bye, Podge. Bye, Mr Chalmers.'

'Bye, lads and thanks.' Spike and Vince set off for their homes, pausing now and again to lean against some obstacle that would hold them up. They hadn't laughed so much in ages.

Podger was helped inside by his Dad. He sat him down in the kitchen chair. His concerned mother appeared from the other room.

'Is he alright?'

'The lads said he had the tooth out.'

'Was it gas you had, Robert?'

'No Smum, snos sneedle.' Podger rose from the chair and went to the sink where he drank greedily straight from the tap, the cold water causing the pain to return.

'Are you hungry? Will I make you something?'

'No shanks, um soft to ped!'

Chapter Nine
1970. Spike gets a Car.

Owning your own car was high on the list of priorities. One by one, the gang from Berrydale were abandoning their bicycles and the contest was on to see who would be the first one to pass the driving test. They tried to save money at every opportunity. Harry and Vince worked overtime, giving them the advantage over Norman and Podger whose hours were pretty much normal but without the opportunity to earn extra cash. Staying with their parents helped them all considerably, although there was always talk about getting a flat in town to gain more independence. They all thought they would be on the road pretty quickly and able to abandon the bus service they had been dependent on. It was part of growing up in a farming community to always be around vehicles of some sort. The trips to Brodie's in particular had them behind the wheel at an earlier age than most. Brodie had always had the time and patience to let them take a turn on his tractor as he worked the fields. They had become quite proficient in the handling of his old Nuffield. Even Wendy had become quite skilled in the steering of the tractor, although she wasn't quite up to working the gears yet.

Spike was determined to be the first to own his very own motor car but he was well behind the others with any money being saved. Donald, his Dad, still worked on deliveries for the Co-op in the High Street. Spike, who had helped out in the past with the lifting of the cookers, TV sets and radiograms was now a full time employee alongside his Dad. He would have much preferred to lounge about at home and watch TV but his Mum had put her foot down and insisted that he got off his backside to earn a living. His duties were assisting in the installation of TV sets, cookers, washing machines and radiograms. It was hard work at times, especially if he and his father had to lift an automatic washing machine up the stairs in a tenement building. The Hotpoints were the heaviest followed by the Belling cookers. Donald did most of the installation work, including wiring. Spike got rid of the cardboard boxes back to the van along with the wheelbarrow and then he would return to look as if he knew what he was doing. Donald was allowed to take home the Thames van that he used at work and Spike had been promised to get to drive it, but he would have to be legal first. It made him all the more determined to get through his test as soon as possible. He had his application for a provisional licence posted off on his seventeenth birthday and as soon as it arrived in the post he applied to sit his test. His choice was Burnside rather than the town. The roads were quieter and he knew his way around. The reply came quicker than he had allowed for. He told his Dad they wanted him for the test in two weeks' time and Spike asked how he would be able to get in some practice. Donald agreed to take him out in the Co-op van but only after clearing it with the area manager. Donald explained that his son would be of much better use if he could do some of the driving from time to time. He knew the routine and the Co-op branch would be more efficient with the additional driver available. The area manager agreed and it was a very happy Spike who popped into Halfords for his L plates.

The next two weeks passed with Spike at the wheel for most of the time. Even in town he was allowed to drive the van on the delivery route. The Thames had a three speed column gear change. The smaller van had four forward gears. When they didn't have a full load, Donald and Spike would take the smaller van round town and it was decided that this was the vehicle in which Spike would sit his test. The day arrived with Spike and his Dad meeting with the examiner at the designated place. The test took about an hour with hardly any traffic about. The emergency stop went well as did the three point turn. They were back at the starting point with an eager-looking Dad waiting for the result. The huge smile said it all. Spike passed and was congratulated on his driving by the examiner who also mentioned that he was his youngest pupil to pass first time. The L plates were removed and the two of them set off back to work to tell everyone the good news. By six o'clock that evening all of Spike's chums had been told as well. They were amazed and it prompted them to get their applications off to Swansea in double-quick time. Over the coming months, after some lessons, Norman passed first time in a school of motoring car. Podger and Vince had to have two attempts. Harry needed three to get his licence. Now the talk was about what kind of car would they all buy. The excitement of having your own vehicle with a girl in the front seat was reaching fever pitch. The conversations started about Jaguars and Rovers and eventually got round to more practical modes of transport.

Spike was still on a mission to be the first on the road with his own wheels. With the help of his Dad he eventually picked up an old Zephyr and spent the first week cruising up and down in the evenings, much to the envy of his chums. He soon realised that by giving them a lift he could get them to help out with the petrol. They were often to be seen in Burnside or in town showing off to any girls they could hunt down. It would be another month before Harry would get a car and Vince would not be far behind. Meantime, Norman and Podger had to be content taking the bus to work. It was still the cheaper option. Spike was certainly having some luck with the girls now that he had a car. He was seldom at home in the evenings. If he was not cruising with the guys then he was off with some impressionable chick to the pictures or a drive in the countryside. The front sliding seat of his Zephyr proved very useful and he would often boast to the rest about his conquests. The petrol bill was proving to be a major outlay for him although it did help that he still went to work with his Dad in the Co-op van. He was the number one driver by now. Donald was happy to be in the passenger seat. It gave him plenty of time to read the papers between jobs and to study the race page. He liked a flutter from time to time and he would remind Spike that it was only a bit of fun and there was no need to tell his

Mum about his habit. It didn't matter to Spike. He couldn't have cared less.

*

It was Thursday evening and the five of them were crammed into Spike's car. They'd had a vote and it was unanimous that Burnside was to be the destination. The first stop was the petrol station to fill up. Money was collected from each passenger and they were off. Much to Podger's delight, they parked the car beside the chip shop. This was a favourite meeting place and this evening there was a group of girls leaning provocatively against the wall.

'Hello, girls.'

'Hello, yourself,' one of them cooed, giving them the look with the head slightly tilted.

'Want to come for a spin?'

'They don't want to go anywhere with you shites!' It was the lad they'd had trouble with at the dance hall. He had appeared from nowhere along with four of his mates.

'Look, lads. We don't want any trouble, so just leave it, OK?'

'Leave it, OK, OK, OK,' he mocked. 'Why don't you piss off back to your mammies and take the deaf one with you.'

The girls were giggling and nudging one another at this confrontation.

'Who are you calling deaf, you ugly bastard? Has someone been chopping firewood on your face?'

'OK, you're asking for it you shites, come on then.'

'Get the wagons in a circle,' laughed Spike.

'Look, we can have these arses,' whispered Vince.

'We're not going to take this in front of these girls. I'll have the big one and you lot take care of the others. Kick them in the knee and get them down.'

'Oh fine, no problem,' thought Podger, unconvinced. 'Odd Job has a plan. Maybe Tonto will jump out and help. He must be around here somewhere and if that doesn't work we can always get Skippy to go for help.'

The big one lunged at Vince who neatly sidestepped and caught his leg on the way past. He rolled over and as he was getting to his feet, Vince brought his knee up and under the lad's chin. He was already out for the count before he hit the pavement. The others charged into Harry, Spike and Podger with fists and feet flailing. Norman jumped on to the back of the one who was kicking Harry. The three of them could be seen spinning around like some dance troupe. Podger, remembering the pep talk from a few minutes earlier, kicked the leg from under his opponent and as he went down he smacked him clean on the chin with his fist, which meant there were now two on the ground. The girls were cheering for the home team, jumping up and down in a frenzy. This support was not working. Another was dispatched by Vince who had pulled off a lad who was getting the better of Spike. This made the contest more even. Now it was Norman who triumphed. He landed a kick to another lad, causing him to shout, 'Enough, enough!' The one lad remaining was rolling on the ground with Spike. It was all over when Spike kicked him between the legs. The girls had stopped cheering by now. They had seen their heroes defeated in battle.

'All right, we've had enough, you win,' was uttered

from someone on the ground. Spike had to have a final kick at his opponent just for good measure. Vince looked at him casually and sighed. 'What took you so long?' The lads who had won the fight at The Burnside Arms could now only crawl away sheepishly, licking their wounds. The girls had gone very quiet as they stood there chewing gum.

'That'll teach the shites,' said Norman.

'If any of you girls want to go out with real men sometime, give us a shout,' said Spike. He would be back very soon, on his own, in the Zephyr.

'Mmm,' they cooed.

'Right, are we ready for some chips?'

'Oh, for Christ's sake, Podge!'

*

Vince and Podger were back at Lucy's house. Her parents were out at the Legion. Now that Lucy was seventeen, her Mum and Dad knew that their daughter was becoming more independent and didn't want to be around her parents all the time. Since she had started going to the college in town, Lucy had been coming home less and less. This was fine with Lorna and Micky. They knew they had a fine daughter, a little head-strong maybe, but generally speaking they were pleased with the outcome. Lucy had started to share a flat with two other girls in town and as far as they knew their little girl was no different from any other young woman of that age. She had the odd boyfriend here and there. The parents never really met any of them which was a comfort in some ways. 'She'll be more interested in her studies, not much time for boys,' they agreed. They knew that she still liked to hang out with Vince and the rest of the bunch and those rascals would always keep a look out for their loved one.

'You want a drink?'

'Have you got some?'

'I have a bottle of wine in my room.'

'Have you any lager?' asked Podger.

'I'll get one of Dad's cans from the fridge. He won't mind.'

'Odd Job. What about you?'

'I'll have a lager as well, if it's OK. I said I'd meet Spike later so I'm not staying long. I'll just have the one.'

'Got anything to eat?'

'Podge, for goodness sake, you and your stomach!' Lucy went off to get a bottle of Liebfraumilch that was stashed in her room. She made a detour past the kitchen to collect the cans of beer.

'Cheers.'

'Look, I have to go,' said Vince, gulping down the contents.

'Give us a minute, I'll come with you.'

'Naw, you finish your drink, Podge. I have to go.'

'Maybe he's scared to be left alone with me,' said the wine drinker.

'Could be. I'm off to meet Spike. I'll see you both later,' Vince said as he walked to the door.

'You got a girlfriend yet, Podge?'

'Yeah...sure I do.'

'What's her name?'

'Well, I haven't anyone special...you know...just playing the field,' he lied.

'Have you done it yet?'

'What?'

'Come on, you know what I mean.'

'Yes, of course I have,' he replied, feeling his face reddening.

Lucy put down her glass and was now standing over Podger who was lying flat on the sofa. He found it difficult to take his eyes off her legs. The short skirts that all the girls were wearing now in the seventies, showed off legs that seemed to go on forever.

'You think I have nice legs?' Lucy asked, pulling up her skirt to reveal more of her beauty.

'You've always had the best legs, and you know it,' he stuttered.

'You want to see more?'

'Oh, come on, what are you going to do? Flash your knickers again like you did at school. We've all seen them.'

'You haven't seen this,' she teased, rolling her skirt up in her hands.

'Lucy! What are you doing?' he heard himself croak.

She was writhing slowly above him in a provocative way. He thought that he was imagining this...a gorgeous young girl who could have any boy she wanted. Lucy continued moving her hands up and down her legs, taking slower strokes on the inside. Her eyes were dreamy, her breathing spasmodic. Her lips were dry...she had to wet them. Now her skirt was way above the tops of her thighs.

'I'm not wearing any knickers...would you like to touch me?' She had moved very close to him by now and, spurred on by the wine, she found she could not stop herself. Lucy had always felt a bit sorry for this fat boy who was continually teased about his weight. She thought he was very handsome and had turned out to be a nice person and felt it was down to her to do something special for him. She suddenly realised that what was unfolding was as exciting for her as it was now apparently for Podger, who had gone very quiet with a very strange tingling in his very dry mouth. She straddled him and guided his hands to where his eyes had been glued for quite a while.

'Oh my god,' he thought. He was shaking badly by now. It was an uncontrollable feeling which he had never experienced before. There were things happening elsewhere that he had experienced.

'Stop shaking,' she whispered as she started to unbutton his trousers. 'If you don't stop shaking, you'll spoil it.'

'Stop shaking,' he thought. 'Don't spoil it...please don't spoil it.' She had him in her hand and was guiding him to a place that he thought he would never get to visit. With a downward thrust she sighed and moaned with pleasure.

'Make it last, please make it last,' she whispered, grinding her body into his groin. She stopped every now and again. She seemed to know the precise moment to pause, holding her virgin partner from his ultimate experience. She had a way of stopping the fluid that was trying to leave the body of the person underneath. 'Stop for a moment,' she gasped.

'No, no!' he cried, but she had dismounted and was removing her top and once more his hands were being drawn to her body.

'Squeeze me!' she cried again, mounting him for the final furlong. This time she did not hold him back. She was ready for her pleasure and she knew that he was long overdue to join her. He thought he heard her scream somewhere in his dream as the two of them reached their goal. 'Was that good? Don't you dare tell anyone.'

He could not speak. He was shaking. He was now a man. He was hungry.

*

'What time did you leave Lucy's? Did you drink all the wine?' asked Vince. Podger had a different look about him today. He seemed to be taller than usual and was sporting a stupid grin.

'Oh...I left just after you,' he replied, turning away, feeling his face changing colour.

'Podge...Podge, were you a bad boy then...you didn't jump her, did you?'

He had been dying to tell them of his visit to heaven but somehow he couldn't bring himself to betray the one who had introduced him to the adult world. In any case, they wouldn't believe him and he would be the butt of more jokes.

'We chatted and drank the bottle. She told me about college,' he lied.

'Did you not try it on with her, then?' asked Spike

'Fuck you! She's a nice girl, not like some of the dogs that you hang around with.'

'All right, all right, keep your shirt on, we're only teasing you. We were only asking.'

'You shites think you know everything.'

'It's OK, Podge. Some take a little bit longer than

others.' They didn't notice the smug look that he was wearing.

'Stupid arses!' he thought.

'Are you coming with me and Odd Job tonight? We're going into the town to the pictures and then the chipper.'

'No, I'll skip it.'

'Loads of chips, Podge, and white pudding.'

'No, I've something else on. I'll see you,' he said, wandering off leaving the two of them bewildered.

'The bugger refused a fry-up!'

Later on, when Vince and Spike were in the Zephyr heading for town, they thought they saw a familiar, fat boy who appeared to be jogging in the opposite direction. They looked at one another...

'Naw, it wasn't, was it?'

'Naw.'

*

Vince had been in the pub a few times with Matthew, starting off with soft drinks but soon progressing to the beer tap. George would turn a blind eye. He knew the lad would soon be eighteen and hopefully a future punter. The same applied to the rest of them. They were gradually drifting in from time to time, slowly acquiring the taste. It made a welcome change from tea and soft drinks.

The young men liked to stand at the bar with the same importance as their parents, listening to the stories being told by the old and wise. An added bonus for them was Victoria. George and Betty's daughter was now spending more time in the bar with the customers, serving meals and drinks, much to Spike's delight. George and his wife had been landlords of the Berrydale pub for as long as the young men could remember. Victoria had been to junior school with the rest of them but she had not been in their company that often. She had also travelled in the school bus to the academy, getting on at a different stop from the rest of them. She was a particularly skinny kid until her final year when she seemed to blossom overnight. Victoria was accustomed to the pub environment and it made sense that she would work full-time when she finished school for good. From the boys perspective she was becoming a very pretty addition to the scenery around Berrydale. If the bar was busy, her mother, Betty, was sometimes behind the counter serving drinks but she preferred to be in the kitchen. It was here that her skills were shown to the full. Her soup and steak and kidney pie were becoming firm favourites with everyone. The pub depended on the local community for its income but people were becoming more adventurous. There was an increase in passing trade, in addition to the odd tourist and the occasional travelling salesman, stopping in past for something to eat. The word soon got around, 'You get a good meal in that Berrydale pub.'

'George, we're running low on steak again!'

*

Spike and Vince were in the car discussing the day's events and the *Carry On* film they had seen at the pictures the previous day. They stopped talking when they noticed the fat figure approaching, jogging and puffing his way up the hill towards where they were parked. Podger had a new pair of trainers on and a red face to match the shiny track suit he was wearing.

'Look! It's Podge. What the hell is he doing?'

'Hoi, Podge! Are you late for the bus?'

'I'm...I'm...just out...I'm just out for a run,' he gasped, trying to gulp in some air.

'You'll give yourself a heart attack if you're not careful. Are you thinking about becoming an athlete or something?'

'Naw, I'm...I'm just trying to get fitter.' He had his hands on his knees, the sweat pouring down his face.

'What's brought this on? You'll do yourself an injury.'

'Maybe. You haven't anything to drink, have you?'

'Yeah, have some of this juice,' said Spike, handing the bottle out of the car window.

'Thanks.'

'Are you wanting a lift home then? You look knackered.'

'Naw, I'm fine. Just need to get my breath back. I'll be OK in a minute.' He took another swig from the bottle.

'Please yourself. We're thinking of going into town later tonight. Fancy coming along? Have you had your tea yet?'

'You two go yourselves. I'm busy stocktaking tomorrow. I'd better be off. See you later.' He went away jogging, leaving the two of them shrugging their shoulders. Podger was gasping for air again by the time he arrived at his front door.

'Is that you, Robert?'

'Yes...yes, Mum, it's me.'

'Supper's ready.'

'I'll...I'll just have some toast...yeah, some toast.'

'Are you feeling OK? Are you serious about this running lark? I hope you're not doing yourself any harm with all this exercise.'

'Yes...yes, I'm fine. Christ, I'm hungry,' he thought. 'Toast will be fine, Mum.'

'We could go to the match on Wednesday, if you like,' said Spike. Vince and Spike were still in the car.

'Who's playing?'

'I think it's the Rovers. It should be a good game.'

'OK, we'll ask the others. When's your birthday?' asked Vince.

'It's on Saturday. I've told the rest of them to be at the pub. I'm not bothered about going into town. Will you mention it to Double Sandy?'

'Yeah, sure, she'll come along. What about Wednesday, then?'

'We'll take my car. You lot can help out with the petrol.'

'What do you think Podge is up to...think he's trying to lose weight?'

'Well, he is a bit fat, isn't he?'

'Yeah, but he's always been a bit plump. We'd better go. If we're going for a cruise tonight, I'll pick up Harry and Norman first then I'll come past for you in about an hour,' said Spike.

'OK, it must be teatime. Come on, let's go home.'

At quarter to seven they were settled in the Zephyr, having had a whip round for the petrol.

'Is Podge coming?' asked Norman.

'Naw, he says he's stocktaking tomorrow. We saw him earlier. He was out running.'

'What do you mean, running?' asked Harry.

'You know, running as in not walking.'

'Why, was someone chasing the bugger?'

'No, he had the track suit and trainers, says he wants to get fitter.'

'You mean, fatter!'

'No, fitter, that's what he said, wasn't it, Spike?'

'Yup, that's what he said.'

'Well, well, life's full of surprises. He'll be going out with girls next.'

'Maybe he already has. He was with Lucy the other night. You saw the look on his face the day after.'

'Lucy! No way. She's a bit too tasty for him. She gets lots of attention from all the boys. Why would she be interested in a fat bugger like him?'

'Oh, who knows. Anyway, let's get going, Spike. We've paid the money...let's fill up with petrol and hit the town.'

After they filled up, they cruised the High Street twice but nothing much was happening. It was on the third pass that Spike stood on the brakes.

'What is it?'

'Look!'

'What?'

'Over there.' He was pointing as he reached for the door handle. The others followed. They were at a loss as to what had grabbed his attention. They assumed he had sniffed out some girls. Spike could find a member of the opposite sex through ten feet of concrete. He had a nose like a bloodhound.

'Where are they?'

'Who?'

'The girls, of course.'

'Never mind about girls. Look at this.'

They were all on the other side of the street by now, staring at what had got Spike in such a state. Parked in a row of cars was a brand-new, gleaming, white Triumph Stag.

'Isn't that beautiful? Doesn't that blow your skirt up?'

'Yeah, that's gorgeous,' agreed Harry, running his hand over the curved lines.

'Look at the steering wheel and the seats.' Spike was drooling over this new piece of machinery. He couldn't have been more excited had he been surrounded by a bevy of girls, all wanting his attention.

'Wonder how much it costs?' Norman asked.

'It'll be a few hundred quid at least. It's almost as nice as a Jag.'

'Well, come on, are we going to stand here all night? It's getting late, let's get back.' They all headed back to where the Zephyr was parked, all except Spike who was still staring at this wonderful car.

'Hurry up, Spike! If you're going to make love to it, will you get a move on, we're wanting home.' The talk on the journey back to Berrydale was of girls and cars, with Spike giving the latter priority over his specialist subject.

'I'm gonna have a red one.'

*

On the Wednesday, they parked the Zephyr in the car park and then found a place in the stand. The game had started. The team from town was playing the Rovers. Both teams were in the same division and doing quite well, not that any of the lads particularly cared. They were not big football fans but it was something else to talk about apart from girls, cars and work. The game had been mildly exciting with the final score two all. They had cheered on the home team in the usual way with the odd bit of advice for the players and the referee.

'Go on, you big lump of shite. Score, you donkey. You got two left feet or something?'

'Aw, come on ref, are you blind or what? That was a penalty. Come on, number seven, I could do better myself.' The game finished and they made their way back through the crowd to the car park.

'Are we going for a drink?'

'Yeah, let's go to The Prince Albert and see if there are any girls.'

'Good old Spike, I knew you wouldn't let us down.'

'Well, have you a better suggestion?'

'Naw, The Prince Albert it is. Are we all agreed?' They all agreed and ten minutes later they were at the bar.

'Hello, Gerry, how's it going?' They had started drifting into this establishment some time back when Vince and Harry had arrived at the legal age for drinking. They now considered themselves regulars. The Prince Albert was near the town centre. It was becoming a popular stopping off place, before moving on to some other pub. There always seemed to be something happening, anniversaries or birthday parties or just groups of people stopping past for a chat.

'Have you lads been to the match? Was it a good game?

'Nothing special, they drew two all. Get us four pints of lager will you, Gerry.' They elected to sit at one of the tables rather than stand at the bar. Spike was eagerly looking around to what was available in the female form.

'How's work then, Harry? Built any mansions lately?' asked Spike.

'I'm working over at a house in Burnside just now. We're building an arbour for this posh woman who is stinking rich.'

'She'd have to be. How many ships has she got?' Spike wasn't quite sure what Harry meant and he didn't want to show his ignorance.

'You know what an arbour is, don't you? What about you, Norman?'

'Sure, we all know what it is.' Norman didn't know what Harry was on about but he wasn't going to be the one to ask. He took enough stick because of his hearing problem. Let some of the others look stupid for a change.

'It's a sort of alcove that you build in the garden,' Harry continued. 'We're going to be there for a few days. You should see the size of this woman's back garden. It's bloody huge!'

'It would need to be for God's sake, some of them ships can be quite big. Have you got the contract to build the canal as well?' They were slipping into the silly mode and they'd only had the one pint. 'That would be a good job for you, digging a canal all the way to the sea shore.'

'Yup, that would keep you busy,' said Norman, entering into the spirit of things.

'Very funny, whose round is it? I got the last ones in.'

'I'll get them,' said Norman, standing up. 'Same again?'

'Yeah, and get us some crisps, will you?'

'You had three pies at the match, Spike. You're getting

as bad as Podge. He hasn't half got serious about this running lark. He's jogging in the morning as well before he goes to work, silly bugger!'

'Maybe he's trying to impress Susan. Have you noticed that he always gets more ice-cream than the rest of us?'

'Same again is it, Norman?'

'Yeah, please Gerry, and four bags of crisps.'

The bar was quiet that evening. It was normally busier at the weekends. While Gerry was pulling the pints, Norman had a look round the bar to see if he could see any familiar faces. Apart from old Woody, he didn't recognise anyone. Woody was in his usual chair, propped against the bar, having a drink with some locals. Woody did odd jobs around town which gave him money for the occasional drink. Tonight he was talking to an American couple who were listening intently to what he was telling them. Norman strained to hear some of the conversation.

'This is a wonderful country that you have...just beautiful. I just cannot find the superlatives,' enthused the Yank.

'There you are, Norman, four pints and four bags of crisps.'

'Thanks, Gerry,' said Norman, handing him a five pound note. He had enough change in his pocket but Norman was still trying to get to grips with the changeover from pounds, shillings and pence. The others were gradually getting used to the different coins they were now dealing with, not that any of them would admit to being confused with the new currency. They were not about to look stupid. There were quite a lot of pound and five pound notes handed over when a purchase was being made, usually resulting in a pocket bulging with change. There was always an opportunity for some leg-pulling on these occasions.

'You must have change in your pocket,' someone would say.

'I'm saving it for the money jar at home,' was a popular reply.

'About time, Norman, what kept you?'

'Get them yourself next time then, Spike. Here's your crisps. Catch.' Norman was studying the change in his hand from the round he had just bought. 'I miss not having half-crowns,' he thought.

'What's the problem? This new money lark is easy. Are you all stupid or something?'

'Yeah, yeah, Spike, empty your pockets. How much loose change have you got in there?'

'Who's the loud bloke talking to Woody at the bar, Norman?'

'Don't know, some Yank whose looking for his relatives, I think.'

'Hey, wouldn't it be a laugh if he was related to Woody?'

'Yeah, that would be funny.'

'For all we know, Woody might have a tin stuffed with money under his bed.'

'I hope for his sake he hasn't got a lot of half-crowns in it.'

'Do you think he's ever had a full-time job?'

'Someone said he was in the navy.'

'You should know, Harry. You must have built some

arbours for the navy? They've a lot of ships, you know.'

'You all set for your birthday on Saturday, Spike? Does Gerry know that we're drinking with an under-age hooligan?'

'I'm sure he does. He never asks my age anyway.'

'Odd Job, do you remember your eighteenth?'

'Very funny, it was only a couple of months ago.'

'Yeah, Double Sandy bought you a cake, didn't she? I remember there were eighteen candles on it.'

'Well, there was on my slice,' laughed Spike.

'Bugger off,' said Vince, pouring the remaining crisps over Spike's head. 'Come on you lot, drink up, we have work tomorrow.'

Chapter Ten
1971. Spike has a Birthday

'Happy Birthday, Spike. What's it like to be legal?'
'No different, George.'
'You better have this one on me.'
'Cheers, am I not getting a kiss, Victoria?'
'Just a peck, then. No nonsense.'

Spike had arranged that historic day at the local. Harry was already there and on his second pint. Apart from Wendy, Spike was the last of the bunch to reach the grand old age of eighteen. Podger wouldn't be coming. He was still on his diet and running as often as he could in the evenings and weekends. Norman arrived next with Wendy and some birthday cards. Vince was at the bus stop to meet Alex. Pamela said that she could stay over and sleep in Grandma's old room. The kitty was set up and the drinks ordered just as Vince arrived with Alex. She had brought Spike a particularly rude card which he accepted with glee. The small talk was mostly about work.

'Who's getting them in?'
'Let's all start calling each other an Indian name based on the last thing that we do.'

'Whaddya mean?' someone asked.

'Well, for example, Wendy could be called, Sipping Orange Juice, George could be, Pulling Pints,' said Spike.

'Oh yeah, and what would Victoria be called?' asked Vince, noticing that she had just adjusted her bra strap.

'Heaving Breasts,' offered Spike.

Harry had wandered back from the toilets. 'What are you all laughing at? Did I miss something?'

They started to giggle.

'Oh hello, Just Been For A Piss. No, you didn't miss anything, isn't that right, Sipping Orange Juice?'

'Yeah, you're right, Just Scratching My Arse.'

'I wasn't scratching my arse!'

'Yes, you were, you do it all the time, Spike.'

'Do I? What next? I never noticed.'

Norman and Alex were trying to teach a German couple how to play darts. They had entered into conversation with the pair who were on a motorbike tour of the country.

'Where are you from, then?' asked Norman.

'We are coming from Hamboorg, ja. You know where this is, ja?'

'Yes, we know where it is,' replied Norman, straining to hear what was being said.

'You have been zer, ever, nein?'

'What!'

'My Engleesh is not good, ja.'

'What's he saying, Alex? What's he mean, gotcha, is he taking the piss?'

'My friend here, Norman, is a little deaf, you know, deaf,' said Alex, pointing to her ear.

'Ha, ha, very goot, ha, ha.' He turned to his female companion. 'Sie sagte, dass ihr Freund eine kleine Elfe ist.'

'Nein, nein, Juergen! Ihr Freund ist ein bisschen taub!'

'Oh, I am sorry. I sot you said he was a little, how you say...elf!'

'Bloody hell,' thought Alex, 'I've got two of them at it now. Look, would you like a drink? You know...drink.' She gestured with her hand.

'Ja, ja, beer.'

'Norman, go and get them a couple of lagers out of the kitty.'

'Goot, goot, beer, ja. What is kitty?'

'We have a cat that pisses beer into a glass, it's quite nice really.'

'Norman!'

'A bit warm sometimes.'

'Norman!'

'You get a good froth on it.'

'Norman, stop being silly in front of these people.'

'Well,' he muttered under his breath as he went to raid the kitty on the table. 'They should learn to speak properly.'

'Are you getting the drinks, then? Just Speaking To Himself.'

'What!'

'Is my squaw winning at darts?'

'What are you going on about? Is everyone going bloody mental?'

While helping Norman at the bar with the drinks, Vince explained the rules of the game that Spike had invented.

'Who's the couple you're playing darts with? I haven't seen them before.'

'I think they're from outer space. I'm sure the bloke's taking the piss.'

'Well, give us a shout if you need any help.'

Norman handed the drinks to the couple and was back with his own beer and a vodka and orange for Alex.

'Danke, prost.'

'Cheers.'

'Are we playing this game or what? Three o one is it? Double start.'

'Your friends drink lots of beer, ja?'

'Ja, Spike will have a hangover tomorrow.'

'He is going to Hanover in Germany...tomorrow, ja?'

'Bloody hell! Alex, you explain. I'm off to the toilet.'

'Calm down, Norman. I'll throw first, hurry up.'

Norman came back past the table where the rest of them were sitting.

'Hi there, Just Speaking To Himself, who's winning?'

'We haven't started yet. Alex is explaining the rules to Big Chief Shit for Brains.'

'You ready for another drink?'

'Yeah, set them up and you better get a couple of beers for the aliens.' Victoria and Spike brought the drinks over to the darters.

'Danke schoen, prost.'

'Cheers.'

'So where have you two come from?' asked Spike, addressing the strangers.

'We are from Germany on holiday. My name is Heidi

and zis is my boyfriend Juergen. Sank you for zee beer from zee pussycat.' Norman and Alex started to get the giggles.

'Am I missing something, Norman? What are you and Double Sandy finding so funny? What's this about a pussycat?'

'Oh, for goodness sake! We're going to be here all night. We'll never get this game going. The pussycat is the kitty, you know...*kitty!*'

'Oh, I get it, Just Chalking the Board...' Victoria left shaking her head.

'What are you on about now, Spike.'

'I'll explain, Alex. That's your Indian name,' piped up Norman.

'My Indian name! Has my Odd Job abandoned Tonto again?'

'I'm off back to the table. Give us another fiver to put in the pussycat, will you?' said Spike.

'Why have you got wiz too many names? I sot you were called Alex and zen you are zis Dooble Sunday?' enquired a puzzled Juergen.

'It's because I'm good at darts. You know, the doobles...I mean the doubles that I was explaining to you earlier on, before the whole bloody world went mad,' answered Alex. She couldn't even contemplate trying to give a reasonable or sensible reply, and anyway, Norman could do nothing for laughing and was choking on his drink.

'I do not understand zis customs you have.'

'Join the bloody club. Right, nearest the bull?'

'Zee bull?'

'Oh, for fuck's sake!'

The game took quite a while with Alex and Norman winning best of three. By the end of the evening they had all ended up drunk, were the best of pals and could speak goodness knows how many languages. The foreign couple had even managed to put some money in the pussycat. They would have a quality hangover tomorrow. The Germans bade their farewells.

'Auf wiedersehen, und, danke schoen.'

'Yeah, yeah, donkey shite, donkey shite,' they replied in a drunken stupor.

Chapter Eleven
1974. Vince goes on Stage.

'Come on, let's go in past the Legion, there's a band on from down south.' Spike, Harry and Vince marched up to the bar. The bingo was still being called.

'Three and nine...thirty-nine.'

'Three pints of lager and a bag of cheese and onion, please.'

'Shh!'

'On its own...number five.'

'Where do you fancy going after this?' asked Spike.

'Shh, be quiet!' shouted another bingo lover.

'Key of the door...twenty-one...six and seven...'

'Thirteen!' Harry shouted, laughing.

'Quiet, at the bar, please!' The natives were hostile.

'Legs eleven...'

'House!'

'Thank goodness, we can speak now, can't we?'

'Yea...'

'Shh! Right, check the card,' shouted the caller to his mate on the floor. Finally it was all over, with some old biddy winning the vast fortune of three pounds.

'Another four scampi!' Bill shouted as he rushed past to the bar.

'Who was that masked man?' laughed Harry, swigging his pint.

'Busy tonight then, Bill?' asked Vince.

'I'm short staffed. I've some down with the flu. Hurry up with those drinks, will you!' he shouted to the overworked barmaid.

'We'd offer you a hand but you seemed to be coping quite well.'

'I don't suppose any of you lads would like to go up and introduce the band? I usually say something over the microphone but I'm too bloody busy right now.'

'Naw, we'll leave that to you professionals.'

'Go on, there's a drink in it for you. I could use some help.'

'Odd Job'll do it,' said Spike.

'Piss off!' replied Vince.

'Go on, we'll get a free drink.'

'Aw, OK, then.' Vince walked up to the stage and picked up the microphone. 'Testing, one...two...testing. Good evening, ladies and gentlemen. Did you all enjoy the bingo, then?'

One or two of them looked up from their scampi in the basket. 'Yes,' was the feeble reply.

'Give us a song, then,' someone shouted.

'Get em off!' came from one of the girls sitting at the table in front of him. 'Show us what you've got!' she giggled.

'Are you girls not having something to eat tonight?' Vince asked.

'No, we're all on a diet,' shouted the blonde one.

'You should try porridge, that'll fill you up. Can you imagine, if it wasn't for Robert the Bruce's wife, we wouldn't have that stuff... *Hey, Robert!*' Vince puts on his best Billy Connolly accent, '*Where ye going? Ye've no had yer porridge!*

I'm no wanting yer porridge, I'm off to Inverness to get they Sugar Puffs.' The girls liked this. '*You can stick yer porridge up yer arse. I'm no wanting it! And while I'm there, I'm gonna go to the Co-op and get a pint o' milk. I'm sick o' milking that goat.*

But Robert, you always have your porridge.

I'm no wanting it. I'm gonna try some of that Weetabix as well for the lads. See if we can win a battle around here. I'm no wanting yer porridge.' The girls and the rest of the crowd loved it.

'Anyway, ladies and gentlemen, please put your hands together and give a warm welcome to...*The Duke Boys.*' The band started up and Vince left the stage to thunderous applause.

'Bloody hell, Vince!' said Bill, hurrying over. 'You want a job?'

'Very funny, get the drinks in.'

'No, I'm serious, look at them.' The crowd was now in good spirits. The dance floor was beginning to get busy.

'What about it, can we talk later?'

'Don't be stupid, where's that drink?'

The Duke Boys were bashing out song after song. The lads were downing the pints. Spike was on the floor doing his stupid dancing with any girl that would join him. Bill had caught up a bit and was having a short break. He poured himself a beer and got them in for Vince, Harry and the silly dancer.

'Well, what about it?'

'What about what?'

'How about that job? I'm serious.'

'Aw, come on, Bill, it was just a bit of fun, just a lark.'

'Look, Vince, the crowd thought that was funny. Do you think you could get them going like that every week?'

'Dunno, I suppose so. What are you suggesting?'

'If you were to come in every Saturday and do a routine after the bingo, there would be a couple of quid in it for you.'

'Just how exactly would that work? I usually go out and enjoy myself at the weekend.'

'Let's say that you were to stand up and say a few words to get the crowd going, then you introduce the band and when they have their break at half-time, you go up again. What do you say?'

'Naw, it's not worth a couple of quid. It doesn't even pay for a night out.'

'OK, OK, what if I say I'll give you a fiver and see how you get on. If it works out, I'll throw in a drink.'

'Can we have a drink as well?' Harry was listening intently to the conversation.

'Bugger off! You think I'm made of money?'

'What are you all talking about?' Spike was back from the dance floor having acquired the phone number of a pretty, young brunette.

'Bill's offering Odd Job some work.'

'Doing what?'

'I was just saying to Vince that I think he would be

quite good doing what he did earlier. I'd pay him as well.'

'If he doesn't do it, I will. Wait till you hear me.'

'Spike, sit down and drink your pint,' Harry said.

'So, what about it, Vince?'

'Alright, I'll give it a go. If it doesn't work out, then there's no harm done.'

'Great, fine, we'll see you next Saturday then. I'd better be getting back.'

'Yeah, yeah, see yah later, Bill.'

'Are we staying here or what?'

'Might as well, the talent's quite nice,' said Spike.

'Did you tell Norman that we'd be here, Odd Job?'

'I spoke to him earlier on. He said that he was feeling tired. He's looking a bit peeky.'

'Peeky?'

'You know, white-faced. He thinks he's got the flu.'

'It's probably with working in that office. It can't be healthy working in that stuffy place with all those folk. No wonder he's got the flu. How's he getting on with that girl typist?'

'Dunno, Spike, he's never said. He seems to be quite keen on her. I think they've been to the pictures once.'

'He's never mentioned it, the sneaky bugger. Wait till I see him next.'

The night wore on. Last orders had been called and The Duke Boys had finished their last number. The crowd all stood up while they played *God Save the Queen*.

'Come on then, everyone,' shouted Bill. 'We all need our beauty sleep.'

'Yes, and some need it more than others,' was shouted back.

'Goodnight, lads.'
'Night, Bill.'

*

It rained that Wednesday. Vince set off with his workmates, Charlie and Wilf, to cut the grass. They started off at the roundabout at James Street and worked their way down to the top of the High Street, making sure that all the verges were neat and tidy.

'Have we to finish all of this today? Why does it always rain when we're on grass cutting duty? Do you think we'll get it done by half-past four?'

'Yez, if we gez a move on.' They hoisted down the mowers from the back of the van and set about the day's work. By twelve o'clock they had most of it done. The grass cuttings were proving harder to rake than normal. They seemed to stick everywhere, particularly on the soles of their wellingtons. The three of them were glad that the council provided them with waterproof jackets and leggings, although a fair amount of water seemed to make its way down the back of their necks. The lunch break was looked forward to on this damp day. Sandwiches were eaten in silence as the three of them sat in front of the van.

'That's better,' said Vince, breaking the silence. 'I needed that. I think I'll pop along and see Double Sandy.' He cleaned his wellingtons and removed the jacket and leggings, tossing them in the back seat. 'I won't be long.'

'Sez you later.'

'Hello, you gorgeous, beautiful creature, have you missed me?'

'Odd Job, you look like a drowned rat. Is it raining?'

'No, I got wet when I jumped in the river to rescue a boatload of people who were in distress.'

'What dress? Have you started wearing dresses now? I worry about you. You're not going over to the other side, are you? It's that Tonto, isn't it? I always knew that he was strange. Never trust a man with a headband. Can I have one last chance to convince you?'

'I know I haven't been in touch. What are you doing on Saturday?'

'I'm busy, Donny Osmond phoned. He's been pestering me all week. I suppose I could stall him. Why? We're not actually going out on a date, are we? The south of France, ah, I've always fancied the Riviera.'

'Alex! Will you shut up for a moment! Blimey, I remember when I could hardly get a word out of you. You haven't had a twin sister all these years, have you?'

'Oh, the game's up. Still it was nice while it lasted. You might as well know now. My name's Ruby. My sister Alex is locked up in the cupboard at home. She's very boring.'

'Alex, for God's sake. I haven't got long.'

'Oh, my prince, you're dying. Why didn't you say? Let me make passionate love to you one last time before you go to that great council building in the sky. If Tonto comes along with you, I'll kick your arse!'

'Alex!'

'Right, I'll go out with you providing I can have you all to myself. Leave all your mates at home, and the Indian and the horse. Where are we going?'

'Eh, well, I thought you might come to the Legion with me.'

'Oh, you're so romantic. We're running off to join the Foreign Legion. Long nights under a Moroccan moon, creepy crawlies in the desert, sand up my arse. I am so lucky to have found you, Odd Job. Donny, you're history!'

'I've to be in the Legion on Saturday. I've a job to do.'

'I thought they cut their own grass?'

'I said I'd introduce the band.'

'Why, don't they know each other?'

'Alex! Stop the funny stuff for a moment. Bill wants me to do something after the bingo.'

'Collect the cards?'

'Look! Are you coming or what?'

'No, I'm a bit hot and squirmy but you're not that good kemosabe. Yes, I'll be there. Now bugger off! I'm busy.'

'I'll see you there then, bye.'

'Yez back then. How's yez bird?'

'Fine,' chuckled Vince. 'She's a bit quiet today.'

*

The word had got around, not surprising when you had mates like Spike and Harry. They arrived at the Legion early to get one of the big tables. Spike was there with Harry. Podger bumped into Alex as she was getting off the bus.

'Hi, Alex, are you coming to the Legion as well?'

'Hello, Podge, I haven't seen you in ages. Bloody hell, you've lost a lot of weight. I'd heard that you were on a health kick. How much have you lost?'

'About a stone and a half so far but I've still got a fair bit to go yet. How's work?'

'It's OK, I suppose. And you?'

'Same. Are you here on a date?'

'I said I would meet Odd Job. Where is he anyway, grooming his horse?'

'What!'

'Nothing, I suppose everyone'll be here. No chance of a romantic evening with my fellow. What's this about him and the band? He's not going to sing, is he? God help us, I suppose we'll find out soon enough.'

They went inside and sat down with the others who were already there. The drinks started flowing. Podger was on soda water and lime.

'Go on, have a pint.'

'No, I'm fine, really.'

'Where's Norman?' asked Alex.

'He's got the flu,' replied Spike. 'I spoke to his Mum. He's off work. Mrs Halford got the nurse to have a look at him.'

'She didn't stick that thing up his arse, did she?' They all laughed as they recalled the long gone days of constipation.

'I remember when Odd Job had it done. Where is he anyway?'

'He should be along shortly... or at least he'd better be, or he'll be getting a kick up the arse from me,' said Alex. 'It was you that started calling him that name, wasn't it, Spike?'

'Yeah, I suppose it was. I remember him telling me that the nurse said it was the oddest jobby she'd seen for a while.'

'Can we get off this subject, please?'

The bingo started. It usually lasted about an hour. They all decided to have a go. Much to his surprise, Spike won a house. He wouldn't have noticed had it not been for Alex keeping an eye on his card. The numbers were checked and the winnings were put in the kitty.

'Are you going to carry on working then, Spike, now that you're a rich man?'

'Might buy out the Co-op, that's what I thought. Don't know what I'll do with the other two quid mind you.'

'Blimey, wouldn't it be great if you had your own business? You could please yourself, get someone else to do the work for you.'

'I would lie in bed all day, Podge, and get up at teatime.'

'You would, you lazy arse.'

'Well, wouldn't you? I suppose you'd be out running the whole time. You'd be able to do a few hundred miles a week. There would be nothing left of you by then.'

'Shh!' shouted the bingo caller. 'Eyes down for the final house.'

Vince arrived just as they were playing the last game. He nodded to the gang as he sat down, not daring to speak. He didn't want to upset the bingo lovers by opening his mouth. Bill had already pulled him a pint. The silence was finally over and replaced with the usual chatter and the ordering of suppers. They looked at Podger sipping his soft drink, half expecting him to order two lots of scampi with double chips, but he was chatting away as if oblivious to the food around him. The band was doing a quick sound check and stocking up on the drink that was then placed to one side of the stage.

'You came along to see me then, Alex,' Vince asked.

'I wasn't doing anything anyway,' she whispered in his ear.

'What happens now, everyone? Odd Job, are you going to sing or do impressions or magic? Go on...give us your bird impressions.'

'What! Are you going to eat worms?' piped up Harry, guzzling his pint.

'Shut up, you lot. I'm only going to introduce the band.'

'When?'

'In about five minutes...it's only five to nine.' They were making him nervous. 'Was it because Alex was here?' he thought. He had a strange feeling in his stomach. He had to go over to the bar and down a large whisky to take the edge off, while getting the drinks in for the rest of them.

'Has anyone seen Lucy recently?' asked Spike.

'I was speaking to her not so long ago in C&A's. She's getting on fine at her fancy job with that solicitor.'

'I suppose she has a regular boyfriend now has she, Alex?'

'I don't think so, Podge. She seems to be quite busy with her work...why?'

'Oh, just wondering, you know.'

'You got something you want to tell us, Podge?'

'No, just making conversation.'

'Are you not having a pint? We're a bit concerned about this health kick you're on. You're not a secret SAS agent are you, in training for some mission overseas?'

'No, Odd Job. I'm working undercover for the tax

office. We heard about you doing work in the Legion and not declaring it. They sent me along to check it out.'

'Could have saved you the journey, I'm only getting a pint.'

'Yeah, yeah.'

'So, Podge. How far do you run in a day?'

'Depends...maybe five or six miles.'

'Bloody hell, that means by the end of the week you're over thirty-five miles away. Do you get the bus back?'

'Very funny, ha, ha. You should give it a try. You'll get yourself fit and healthy.'

'I'd rather get my exercise in other ways.'

'Yeah, we've all heard about your expeditions in the Zephyr, Spike. Who's the current bimbo?'

'Still looking for the right one, Harry. Plenty of time yet before I settle down.'

'Has anyone been speaking to Wendy recently?'

'She would have been here tonight, but I think she's on night shift at the hospital.'

'My boss, Mr Simpson does a lot for hospitals.'

'Oh really, Podge.'

'Yeah, he makes people sick.'

'Are you on the instruments full time now?'

'More or less, except when Simpson gets the hump and asks me to help out Molly with the records. I don't mind, she's good fun.'

'Is there any chance of a romance there? She's quite good-looking.'

'Spike, there's more to life than chasing girls.'

'Is there? I suppose you'll be a bit fussy now that you are so slim. I think you've got the hots for Lucy, haven't you?'

'Piss off! Go and get the drinks in. It's your turn to go to the bar before we all die of thirst.'

'OK, OK, same again, everybody?'

'Yeah.'

Spike came back with another round of drinks. He sat the tray down on the table and parked himself back in the seat.

'Spike was saying that Norman has the flu. Have you seen him, Odd Job?'

'I went round past to see if he was coming tonight. He's in bed. If he's not better by tomorrow, his Mum's getting the doctor in.'

'He'll just be skiving for a few days.'

'No, he didn't look well.'

'Hope none of us catch it,' said Harry. 'Mind you, I could do with a few days off work.'

Vince was given the nod from Bill as the hour approached. The band was standing just off stage, having been told there was a new compère tonight. Vince stepped up to the microphone, tapping it to make sure it was on.

'Hello, everyone, good evening. Just before the music starts, I'd like to welcome some people that we have in tonight all the way from Texas. It's good of them to drop in past considering they must be a bit jet-lagged after their flight. So please make them welcome.' The crowd applauded.

A voice from the table shouted, 'Texas Homecare!'

'What!' said Vince, looking puzzled. The crowd chuckled. He paused and looked around waiting for the laughter to subside.

'Texas Homecare?' he asked.

'Yes,' was the reply.

'Right,' he continued, addressing the table. 'Maybe you can tell all of us here the answer to this...What does an assistant from the hardware department look like?' He leaned over to the microphone. *'An assistant from the hardware department to checkout one, please!'* Vince slowly looked left, then right, then left again. The crowd were all ears. The routine was going well. 'Can you imagine being in a pub someday in the back of beyond and there sitting in a dark corner you see a shadow? Hi, so what do you do? you ask.

Shh. Not so loud. I'm an assistant from the hardware department. Keep your voice down.' There was a lot of laughter from the crowd now.

'And, tell me this?' asked Vince, once more addressing the people sitting at the table. 'Why is it when I've just popped in for a bag of nails, I go to the quietest checkout and there in front of me is a woman who is fumbling in her bag for her cheque book to pay for goods worth a pound. *Now who's it made out to?* she will ask.' Vince continued, 'She has more fumbling about to find her cheque card...I've only popped in for a bag of nails for goodness sake!' The crowd nod in approval. They are familiar with this scenario. 'Then...,' he goes on, '...just when I think it's my turn, she fishes out of her bag, four rolls of wallpaper. *Can I return these? I have the receipt somewhere...Certainly,* the checkout person will say, leaning over to the tannoy. *An assistant from the hardware department to checkout one please.* Oh for Christ sake!' The crowd now roar with laughter. 'Let's move on now with your band for tonight. Please give a warm welcome to...*The Three of Us.*'

'Bloody hell! Look at him now,' said Spike over the applause. 'He's got them in the palm of his hand.'

'Who would have thought,' agreed Harry. 'There's our Odd Job, on stage, an entertainer.'

'I know. He's come a long way, hasn't he? Good old Odd Job...from short trousers to show business.'

They all laughed. 'Who's getting the drinks in?'

The band was half-way through singing *Jambalaya* when Vince was back at the table having weaved his way through the dancers. Alex was the first to speak.

'Well, well, does this mean you'll be giving up your job fighting the bad guys? What will you do with Silver? Will he be put out to pasture or end up pulling a milk float, poor thing? And what about Tonto? He'll probably go on the unemployment. Who's going to give a job to an out of work Indian? Will he end up in a circus demeaning himself for a crust of bread or a slice of buffalo? He'll look a bit out of place standing in the dole queue in his moccasins.'

'You're mad, Alex, but I quite like you.'

'I was clapping, especially when you'd finally shut up. Can I have a dance please?'

'Of course, my pumpkin, help yourself.'

'At last, I have you to myself,' she said, snuggling into his neck. 'Can you smuggle me into your room tonight? I want your autograph without the pen and paper.'

'I don't know. My Mum and Dad will hear us.'

'Go on, you can keep your mask on, I won't reveal your identity, but you'll have to take your gun belt off, and your hat.' She kissed him that special way that melted him to jelly.

'Yes, yes, OK, but we'll have to be very quiet.'

'Can we go, now?'

'I can't, I have to go up again at half-time. You know what it's like for us show business people. What if we get to the door and the TV people are there?'

'Keep your mask on, or do that disguise that you do of the old man. That fools me every time I see it on the telly. Does Tonto know it's you?'

'You're crazy, are you ever going to grow up?'

'Never.'

The band finished the slow number and had started another. Alex and Vince were snuggling close together cheek to cheek, almost dancing. Spike had ambushed a girl from a table where she had been sitting with her chums and the two of them were now on the dance floor. The poor girl was having to listen to Spike's chat-up lines.

'Do you like cars?'

'Yes, what do you drive?'

'I've got a Zephyr. It has a sliding front seat, column change.'

'Haven't you got anything better than a Zephyr? I like Jags.'

'Me too, I was thinking about getting one but I could pick you up in the Zephyr any time you like.'

'I hardly know you. One of my friends has been out with you and she says that you're a bit of a lad.'

'Oh well, you know.' Spike took this as a compliment. 'So, what do you say, will I pick you up sometime? We could go for a drive.'

'I'll think about it. Pity you don't have a Jag.' The band finished the slow number and the dancers were making their way back to their drinks.

'Can I have your phone number, then?'

'No, you're too pushy. You've never even asked my name. Besides, I've heard that you and your Zephyr are rubbish...bye.' And with that remark, she went back to her chums who were sitting at the table giggling.

'Oh well,' he thought, 'her loss.'

'What's the matter, Spike, you been stood up?' laughed Harry.

Vince and Alex finally let go of each other long enough for Alex to go to the toilet.

'That was great, Vince, here's your fiver, are you wanting a drink?'

'I'm OK for now, Bill. Thanks for the nod about the girls from Texas Homecare. Who else is here tonight?'

'We've got some taxi drivers in and also some girls from the hairdressers in Burnside. What's it called again?'

'Yeah, I know the one you mean. I'll see you later. I need the toilet.' Vince came back and went on stage for the second-half.

'We'd like to welcome the girls from Freda's hair stylists who are here with us tonight. Hope you all are enjoying yourselves...tell me this...why is it that you girls move around so much?' Vince imitated a phone call. *'Hello is that Top of the Shop?*

Yes this is Top of the Shop. Do you wish to make an appointment?

Yes, can I make an appointment with Sonya, please?

Sonya doesn't work here anymore,
Oh...do you know where she's gone?
I think she's gone to Snips and Clips.
OK, thanks.' He imitates another phone call.
'*Good morning, Snips and Clips, how may I help you?*
Hello, I'd like to make an appointment with Sonya, please.
Sonya doesn't work here anymore.
But I thought that was where she'd moved to?
Oh, yes, she worked here for ages, about two weeks. She moved on to Hair is Us.
OK, thank you.' Vince turned to the crowd in front. 'All you're wanting is your bloody hair cut. It's growing longer by the minute.' He could see the crowd was enjoying this. He carried on. '*Ring, ring.*
Good morning, Hair is Us.
Hello, can I make an appointment with Sonya, please?
Sonya doesn't work here anymore.
Oh...for Christ's sake!'

The crowd yelled and clapped. 'Anyway...welcome back, *The Three of Us.*'

'Does this mean you're finished now, my prince?'

'Yup, just the autographs to sign.'

'Can we not go back to your house now...if you're finished?'

'It's too soon, Alex. My Mum and Dad will still be up.'

'They might be having an early night.'

'It's still too soon, Alex.'

'What time do they go to bed?'

'I know they weren't going out tonight so they'll

probably watch TV and then go to bed.'

'What time?'

'Oh, I don't know. I'll tell you what, we'll go at eleven, OK?'

'You'll be well pissed by then,' she replied.

'And what about you? You're knocking them back, aren't you?'

'Yeah, but it doesn't affect us girls, you know, the way it affects you fellows.'

'I'll slow down. It isn't easy with these drinkers at the same table.'

The time passed quickly with Alex and Vince having a few more dances. The last orders were called. Vince had kept his promise about going easy on the alcohol. The same couldn't be said for Alex. She was in fine form. She seemed to flirt with every man in the hall, much to their delight. She danced all the fast tunes with each male getting a turn. The slow tunes were reserved for Vince who was wishing his parents were away for the night. Alex was teasing him relentlessly as they danced. The rest of the gang sitting at the table were in fine voice by now, rendering a particularly bad version of *Delilah*. It was nearly midnight when Vince and Alex staggered up the road to the house.

'The lights are out, shh!'

They managed to negotiate the stairs to Vince's bedroom without any noise. He helped Alex undress due to the euphoric state she was in. Somehow she didn't seem to mind. 'I hope she doesn't fall asleep on me,' he thought.

Alex had no intention of going to sleep, as Vince was

about to find out. They managed to wake up in the morning in time for her to catch the first bus back to town. She sneaked down the stairs and let herself out without a sound. An hour later Vince met his Dad, having his breakfast, in the kitchen.

'Morning, son, sleep well?'

'Fine, Dad. And you?'

'You must have had quite a dream last night with all that giggling you were doing in your sleep.'

'Eh...was I dreaming?'

'Not half,' was Matthew's reply, trying to hide a grin.

'How did you get on at the Legion last night?'

'It went very well. I got a fiver.'

'A fiver?'

'Yeah.'

'What did you do for that, then?'

'Oh, I just introduced the band...no big deal.'

'Are you doing it regularly?'

'Yeah, I've been asked.'

'Your Mum and I will have to come and see you. A fiver you said?'

'More pressure,' thought Vince.

'Was your girlfriend there? What's her name again?'

'You mean, Alex. Yeah she came along.'

'When are you bringing her round again?' asked Matthew, giving Vince a grin.

'Eh, I don't know. Sometime I suppose. She's a bit crazy.'

'What do you mean? She should be locked up?'

'Nah, she's just daft sometimes. Actually, she's OK.'

'Well, bring her round past. The door is always open,

you know that.'

'I will, Dad, I will.'

'Right, I'm going to give the car a clean. I don't suppose you want to give me a hand, do you, Vince?'

'I'm pretty tired, Dad.'

'I'll bet you are, son. I'll bet you are!'

*

On Monday evening, Vince and Spike agreed to meet in the pub after work. Harry was working overtime on some new building in town that was behind schedule. Spike had arrived first and was on his second pint.

'What are you having, Odd Job?'

'The usual for me, Victoria. And get one for Spike.'

'Put it in the tap for me.'

'Been here long?'

'Just got in. I've had a shite of a day. I shifted two Hotpoints and three Bellings. One of the drops we did, the automatic was right at the top of a bloody tenement. We got all the way to the door and, you'll never guess... the woman wasn't in.'

'Did you hump it all the way down again?'

'Naw, we left it there and went back later. The woman wasn't pleased that we'd left her bloody washing machine at the door. I wasn't going to go back down and then up again with that weight, nearly did my back in just with taking it up the stairs. How about you?'

'Oh, just the usual stuff, nothing new. I thought I'd go and see if Norman's feeling any better. Maybe he wants to come for a pint. He must be over the flu by now.'

'OK, just let me finish this drink and I'll come with you. Remember I've got one in the tap, Victoria. We'll probably be right back.'

'Don't worry, Spike, I won't do you out of your pint,' she replied, fluttering her eyelashes. She enjoyed teasing him. He had asked her many times to go for a drive in his Zephyr but she had no intention of being another notch on his gun-belt. Vince and Spike hopped into the car for the short drive to the Halford's and were greeted at the door by Norman's Dad.

'We came to see how the skiver is. We wondered if he wanted to go for a pint?'

'Come in, lads. I shouldn't think so. He seems to have the flu hanging about him. Come in anyway, he'll be glad to see you.'

'Hello, Mrs Halford, how's the invalid?'

'Hello, Vincent, hello Spike. Come on through, he's watching TV.'

'How are you feeling, Norman, fancy a pint?'

'I'd like to but I can't seem to get rid of this bug.'

'We'll leave you lads to have a chat. Do you want a cup of tea or anything?'

'No thanks, Mrs Halford, we've still a pint in the tap down at the pub.'

'So, you've still got this bug then...you look like shite.'

'Thanks very much. I've had the doctor in. He says I've to go in for some tests.'

'Tests, what kind of tests? It's not to do with your ear, is it?' asked Vince. The people who knew and had grown up with Norman, had learnt to speak slightly louder and more concisely than had they been talking to anyone else. This was something they did without thinking, unless they were trying to wind him up. In which case, they would mutter to themselves to try to annoy him but Norman always took the banter in good fun.

'No, the doctor says it's just routine.'

'Speaking about routines, you should have seen Odd Job on stage at the Legion on Saturday,' said Spike.

'Did it go OK, then?'

'Naw, he was shite, could have done better myself. What's this about you and the typist from the office, you sneaky bugger?'

'We've been out once, that's all.'

'Did you...you know?'

'Maybe, Spike, maybe.'

'Come on, spill the beans, tell your mates.'

'She's a nice girl. She wants to go out on another date. I'll take her out once I get rid of this dammed bug.'

'OK, OK, we don't want to know anyway. So you're not coming for a pint, then?'

'You two go ahead, I'll catch up with you later in the week. Are you still trying to get into Victoria's panties, Spike?'

'One arse hole in there is enough,' chuckled Vince.

'Fuck you, Odd Job! Come on my pint's waiting for me.'

'We'll see you later, Norman. Are you wanting any flowers or chocolates?'

'Piss off the pair of you, unless you want to send round a nurse with big knockers.'

'What about Wendy? She's a nurse.'

'I said *big* knockers.'

'We'll tell her that.'

'See you later.'

'Yeah, bye.'

Harry was propping up the bar by the time they got back. He hadn't been home yet as was evident by his appearance.

'You're starting to look more like Patrick every day. Harry, you're bloody filthy. Have you been working overtime again?'

'Yeah, I've been mixing cement all day. I was gagging for a pint. Have any of you seen Norman?'

'We've just been round past. He's still got the flu hanging about him. The doctor's been in today, he's sending him for some tests.'

'Did you ask him if he's been out with that typist from work?'

'Yeah, he's not telling us very much.'

'I suppose you'll be at the Legion from now on, Odd Job.'

'I'll see how it goes, Harry, the money's handy.'

'Must be your round then.'

'Yeah, same again, Victoria. I don't know about you lot but I'm not staying here all night and getting trashed. I want to have a look at my car. I think the plugs could do with changing and maybe I'll get a chance to give it a good clean as well. I never seem to have the time to do it.' Vince drank his pint and was ready to go and look at his motor.

'I'm off then. Are you two staying, or what?'

'I'm going to go home and get cleaned up after this pint,' said Harry.

'Yeah, we'll see you later, Odd Job. I'm going as well after this one. I'll drop Harry off at his house. Let's have a sensible evening for a change.'

'You off then, Odd Job, is my company not good enough?'

'I'm going home to sort my car. I'll see you Victoria.' It didn't take Vince long to get to his front door. He was eager to get started.

'Vincent! Thank goodness you're home.'

'What's wrong, Mum?'

'Look in the garden!'

Vince did as he was told and opened the back door. One of Brodie's sheep had broken through the fencing and was now having a snack in Pamela's garden. Brodie rented the field, that ran parallel with the Wright's back garden, to graze his sheep. He had herded the flock down a few days before but had been a bit lax in checking the fence.

'It's only one of Brodie's ewes, Mum, what's all the fuss?'

'I want it out of there. It's eating my strawberry plants!'

'Where's Dad?'

'He isn't home yet. Now move that animal before it completely destroys my garden.'

'Aw, Mum, I want to sort my car.'

'Get it out of here now, Vincent!'

Vince gave in to his mother's demands and set foot down the path towards the sheep. It was nonchalantly chewing the strawberry leaves as it looked at the approaching figure. Vince was three steps away from the beast when it decided to make a run for it to the other side of the garden where it was about to continue munching on the herbaceous border. Vince strolled slowly over to the animal. His intention was to corner it and somehow lift it and toss it back in the field. He was within striking distance when it decided to move back to the strawberry plot.

'Vincent! Watch what you're doing, you're scaring it. You'll have all my plants ruined. Can't you catch it?'

'It's not that easy, Mum, I can't get close enough. Can't I leave it until Dad comes home? The two of us will have a better chance.'

'No! Get it out of here now. It's wrecking my garden.'

The ewe dodged Vince once more and was back at the flowers, still munching the contents of the garden.

'It's no use, Mum. We'll never catch it on our own.' Pamela had joined her son in a vain attempt to corner the beast.

'Get a rope from the garage, will you? We'll catch it that way.'

Vince went to the garage to fetch a stout rope his Dad used for all sorts of things, like having the car towed when it would not start. Now he was back facing the bemused creature.

'Well! Make a noose, Vincent, hurry up, will you.' Pamela was getting very distraught at the sight of her vanishing flower bed.

Vince had the slip knot in place and was eager to try his skills in the ways of the Wild West. He had seen this done before in the movies and on TV. His first attempt fell short of the mark, resulting in one scared sheep doing a particularly ungraceful trot through the brassicas.

'Vincent! Now look what you've done.'

'All right, Mum, all right. I'll try again.' This time he managed to slip the noose over the creature's head and as it made to run, the rope tightened. The ewe was not amused and tried its best to escape but Vince was having none of it. He was rather pleased with himself. All he needed now was a stetson and cowboy boots and he would look the part.

'Well! What are you going to do now?'

'Give us a minute, Mum, I'm out of breath. It's too heavy to chuck over the fence. Can't I just tie it up?'

'Don't be stupid. It'll strangle itself. You'll have to take it to the gate and put it back in the field with the rest.'

'But, Mum, that's miles away!'

'It is not! It's only up the road a bit. Now go on, get a move on!'

Vince pulled the sheep behind him and was surprised at how easily it followed. 'Maybe it had eaten its fill,' he thought. The two of them made their way up the road and had just managed twenty yards, when he heard the car pull up behind him. He knew without looking who the driver was likely to be.

'Hoi, Odd Job! If you'd told me I could have got you a Jack Russell or a Cocker Spaniel!' Spike and Harry were both out of the car by now, chuckling.

'What breed is it anyway?' asked Harry.

'It's a sheepdog,' was the reply.

'Is it any good at catching rabbits?' The ewe was standing chewing its cud and looking at the three of them as if it were thinking, 'Who are these buggers that are spoiling my walk?'

'What's its name, Rex or Rover?'

'Shep!'

'Does it do tricks?'

'Yeah, it likes to jump up on the bonnet of Zephyrs and shite all over them. I'm training it to fetch the paper in the morning.'

'It could do with a haircut. It's an overgrown poodle, isn't it?'

'Yeah, if you say so, Spike.'

'Has it got any more chewing gum left?'

'No, that was its last bit, you're out of luck.'

'Where are you taking it, anyway?' asked Harry.

'We're going to the pictures! Where the fuck do you think we're going?'

'It's not *Lassie* that's on, is it? The animal was showing its impatience by now and demonstrated by relieving itself on Spike's shoes. 'How dare they interrupt my walk with my new-found friend!'

'Oh, look what's happened. It's done poo poos on your shoes, Spike. You've hurt its feelings.' Vince was now the one who was laughing.

'Anyone fancy a game of marbles?'

The beast was now bleating for its pals in the field. It looked fed up with all this nonsense.

'It's got a funny bark. Has it got a cold?'

'Will you two bugger off and let me take this thing back to the field. I'm trying to get a look at my car.'

Harry and Spike set off in the Zephyr, still laughing out loud. Vince was anxious to get on with the task before anyone else came along and gave him a hard time. He had to pull the animal along the last few yards as it kept trying to stop and feed on the lush grass at the verge of the road. He managed to reach the gate with difficulty and had to tie it to the fence whilst he opened the wooden obstacle. The others in the flock arrived to see what was happening to the member of their family and on release, the ewe skipped and ran to join them. 'You'll never guess where I've been?' Vince imagined he heard it say.

Chapter Twelve
1974. Norman goes back to Work.

The offices of *The Spokesman* were situated at the edge of town surrounded by a housing estate that belonged to the council. The readership of the paper was spread over a large area. It was the only daily paper that was printed for that part of Scotland. Norman was on the second floor of the two floor building. He was a valued member of staff, assisting in the layout of the news that was then sent to the printing presses on the ground floor. He didn't have a job title as such but was known as an assistant on the second floor. He had started as tea boy and general dogsbody, delivering messages from office to office. He was one of the juniors for a while before being promoted to being an important member of staff. He shared a desk with another colleague which was a workable arrangement. All the staff members liked this cheeky hooligan from the moment that he had started work there and had been quick to adapt to his hearing disability. They had their moments of fun with him, as was expected with working in an office environment, but he always seemed to get the last laugh, due to his background training growing up in Berrydale.

One of the typists had her eye on Norman and it was only after gentle persuasion on her part that they'd finally gone out on a date. Norman had managed to keep it reasonably quiet about his date with Sandra. He didn't know if this was going to be a serious relationship or not and he wasn't about to have her slagged off by his chums until he had some time to get to know her better. Sandra had introduced him to *The Stupid Grin Club*. He'd almost become a member at school but it had amounted to no more than a quick fumble. The serious act had always eluded him until Sandra came along. She had insisted that they get down to business on that first date and who was Norman to argue. In any case, Norman was glad to be a fully fledged member which had taken the pressure off. He had arranged to meet Vince at Antonio's during both their lunch hours to catch up on some gossip.

'You got rid of the flu then?'

'Yeah, I'm feeling better. I've been back to the doctor to get the result of my blood test.'

'And?'

'Well, he spoke to my Mum first. The doc's not happy. He's sending me back for another test.'

'Why, did they lose the first one?'

'No, it's something to do with my blood cells being wrong. My Mum says it's OK. They usually have to do a second test most times apparently. I've got to go back to the bloody hospital in a couple of days. How's work? What have you been up to, Odd Job?'

'Oh, nothing much, you know, just the usual routine. Wilf and Charlie are a good laugh.'

'Have you thought any more about the gold coins?'

'Sometimes. Have you any suggestions?' asked Vince.

'No, can't help there. Are you giving up on them?'

'Might as well forget about the whole damned thing. I thought it was too good to be true. Are you coming in past for a pint sometime? The others are asking about you.'

'Yeah, I've been meaning to come in past but I seem to fall asleep after suppertime these days. I must be working too hard.'

'You're getting old, you bugger, isn't that right, Susan?'

'What are you on about?' Susan had arrived at the table. She had been serving a family with tea and scones. 'Hello, Norman, where have you been hiding?'

'Nowhere, I've been down with the flu. How's things with you. Got a boyfriend yet?'

'Loads of them but I'm really saving myself for you.'

'Now you tell me,' he replied with a slight blush. 'If only,' he thought.

'Are you two having something to eat or are you going to sit there all day talking like a couple of old women?'

'Give me a cup of tea and a bun. What about you, Norman?'

'I'll have the same please, Susan.'

'OK, lads, I'll be right back. How's Double Sandy?'

'How is she, you're asking me *how is she*? She's crazy, that woman...off her bloody head.'

'But you quite like her.'

'She'll do for now,' replied Vince with an affectionate grin. Susan came back with the tea and buns. 'We don't sell as many buns now that Podge has stopped coming in. Is he still running? I haven't seen him for ages,' asked

Susan.

'Yeah, he's still at it, lunch time as well. He's lost a lot of weight and is getting the eye from the girls. I'm sure that's what keeps him going. He's had to throw out most of his clothes. They're too big for him now.'

'He could have given them to Patrick. Tidy the bugger up.'

'Yeah I suppose. We'd better be getting back. It's ten to one. I'll see you later, Norman. You'll be in past the pub sometime now that you're feeling better. Bye, Susan.'

'Cheerio, lads, don't be so long in coming back. It's pretty dull around here now without you lot coming in past.'

For the rest of the week Norman went about his work in the office as usual. He still didn't feel like his old self. The following week he went back for his second test at the hospital. The results were quicker in coming back this time. It was only a matter of days before Mrs Halford and Norman were in the doctor's surgery. They had been sitting in the waiting room for some time and were the last to go through. The doctor had wanted to make sure that he would have enough time with Norman and his Mum to answer any questions that they might ask about the results of the tests. The doctor told them that Norman's white cell blood count was abnormally high and he would have to go to hospital for a further test. Something was not right and this next visit would help them get to the bottom of the problem. The doctor said that he would make the arrangements for Norman to attend as soon as he could and they should expect a letter to arrive in the next few days, instructing them as to the date.

*

'Hello, Norman, what are you doing here?' He bumped into Wendy at the main reception of the hospital.

'I'm here for another test. I can't seem to shake this thing off.'

'Do you know where you're going?'

'Yeah, I've been before. How's things with you?'

'Fine, you know, making up beds, emptying bedpans, wiping arses.'

'I wouldn't fancy your job.'

'It's OK, you get used to it. I enjoy it. It'll do until I meet that handsome millionaire.'

'You didn't fancy following in your father's footsteps then?'

'No bloody way! Religion is fine, but preaching it, no thanks. How's the rest of the riff-raff doing? Are they behaving?'

'I shouldn't think so. We don't see much of you these days. Are you still working these funny hours?'

'Yeah, I do a fair bit. When I finish work, all I want to do is sleep.'

'With anyone in particular?'

'Mind your own business, you cheeky bugger.' Wendy blushed at the suggestion.

'I'm just teasing you. I'm sure you do OK with all these doctors around.'

'Is Spike still trying for a world record? He must have been out with all the girls in the area by now.'

'You know what he's like, Wendy, him and his Zephyr. I'm sure he exaggerates most of the time. We all just humour him. I'd better get going or I'll be late for my appointment. Probably see you around sometime.'

'Yeah, Norman, hope to catch up with you all, soon. See you around.'

Norman had his blood test again along with a full examination. This time he had to give a sample of his bone marrow. They gave him a local anaesthetic before inserting the needle in the area of his pelvis. The whole procedure was over and done with within an hour, resulting in some discomfort on the journey home as the effects of the anaesthetic began to wear off. He was to get the results from his own doctor three days later when he and his Mum sat in front of the desk in the surgery.

*

That December was cold and frosty with the odd scattering of snow. The Christmas holidays were over and there was the turmoil of New Year's Eve to contend with. Now that all the Berrydale bunch were grown up, they looked forward to the end of the year and Hogmanay. Vince was determined to gather them all in one place and have a good time. In previous years, they had enjoyed themselves by staying at home to see in the New Year then moving from house to house, as was the tradition. It was usually sometime next day before they would get back to their respective homes. It was not unusual for the odd straggler to be away for longer if the party was going well.

That New Year everyone arranged to meet up in The Prince Albert, in town, straight after work. Vince finished early along with the rest of the council staff and he was on his third can of lager by four o'clock. He had remembered to take a change of clothes with him and so had most of the others. Matthew raided the petty cash box to make sure there was plenty of drink in the office. He made a little speech to thank them all for the hard work they had done that year and asked everyone present to spare a thought for the men who would be keeping the roads clear with the snow ploughs and gritters. There was never a shortage of volunteers at this time of year because the overtime was just too good to miss. By six o'clock all the employees in the council office were in good spirits. Vince and the others promised to try to look in past Wilf's house sometime during the night.

'If yez gez a chance, yez welcome to come in pazt. Bring yez mates az well.'

'Thanks, Wilf, I'll see how it goes.'

It was half-past seven in the evening before Vince walked through the door of The Prince Albert. The pub was busy with Harry and Podger already seated.

'Are you the only ones here?' asked Vince.

'Yeah, so far. We've started a kitty so get your money in, Odd Job.'

Vince obliged just as Alex and Wendy arrived.

'Hello, you shites, Hello, my prince. Are we missing anything?'

'No, Alex, we've just got here.'

'Then get us a drink. Wendy and me are gagging. Are we all here, then?'

'No, Spike's still to show up.'

'Oh, for Christ's sake, I can hardly wait. What about Norman?' asked Alex.

'He's at home. We can catch up with him later. You

know how tired he gets. How did you manage to get the night off, Wendy?'

'I'm due heaps of time off. I thought, bugger it, let someone else do the holiday shift for a change. I do enough as it is.'

'Good girl.'

'Has anyone spoken to Lucy recently?' Podger asked casually.

'She's going down south to see some of her relatives. I spoke to her briefly last week,' said Wendy.

'We never see her these days. When was the last time that you saw her, Podge?'

'Oh, I don't know, months ago,' he replied, looking rather dejected.

'She wouldn't recognise you now anyway, you skinny bugger. I'm surprised you're not out running tonight. Are you having the night off?'

'Give us a break, will you, I can still enjoy a beer. It's Hogmanay, for God's sake.'

'Hello, everyone, a Happy New Year!' Spike had flown through the door like some aeroplane on its final approach. It looked suspiciously like he'd had a drink or two. 'Hello, you shites, a Happy New Year!'

'Bloody hell, Spike, it's a bit early, we haven't had the bells yet. Sit down on your arse. Where have you been? Have you been home to change?'

'Change...nope. No time to change, been too busy. I'll have a whisky if you don't mind and make it quick, I'm thirsty. Hello, girls, are you all here to see me...am I late?'

'Not late enough. Did you have an office party?'

'Oh yes, did we ever. Someone poured a drink down

the filing cabinet that holds all the records and who did they blame? I plead innocence on the grounds of insanity. Where's my bloody drink?' And with that statement, he slid into a chair. Vince came back with the drinks for the girls.

'I got you a pint, Spike. Try and make it last, will you, you've had enough whisky for now. How do you expect to get through the night? We've a few hours to go yet.'

'Whatever you say, Odd Job, whatever you say.'

'If we're going visiting we're going to need a carry-out,' said Wendy.

'Yeah, you're right. What if we all chip in to the kitty and get what we need?'

'We only need some whisky and vodka. Gerry will sell us that,' said Podger.

'And we'll need some mixers too. We'd be cheaper going to a shop.'

'There's nothing open at this time, is there?' asked Wendy.

'Yes there is. There's that off-licence run by the Chinese couple just beside James Street. I've used it before. It's not far from here.'

'Are you sure it's open tonight, Alex?'

'Yeah, you know that Chinese couple stay open all the time. It'll be open till ten at least.'

'Well, that's settled then...who's going for it?'

'I'll go, Harry,' said Podger. 'Why don't you come with me and help me carry it.'

'That's fine with me. Does anyone else want to come along?'

'No, it's freezing out there. We'll stay here thank you

very much. Why don't you take Spike and sober him up a bit.'

'Good idea. What do you say, Spike?'

'I was just getting comfortable,' he replied with a burp, 'but if you insist, I shall be glad to help you. I need some ciggies. They're too bloody expensive here. Wagons ho!'

'Hang on a minute, Spike. Let's get the money sorted out first.'

'Give us a fiver each and we'll get the rest when me and Podge come back. Do we know what we want?'

'Just get whisky and vodka. Never mind anything else.'

Harry and Podger collected the money and set off with Spike taking up the rear, swaggering along and singing to himself. It took them ten minutes to reach the off-licence. They would have been there sooner if Spike had not stopped to speak to every female who was out and about that evening. They decided to get two bottles of whisky, two of vodka and a half bottle of gin just in case they ran into the Reverend Calder or somebody else who drank that spirit. They bought some lemonade, tonic and Coke. Two stout carrier bags were requested from the oriental shop-keeper who was not amused at Spike's attempts at far-eastern humour. Spike could be heard in the background uttering, *Ah so*, every now and again.

'What your friend want?' asked the shop-keeper.

'Oh, don't mind him. He's just telling you that he's an arse-hole. He gets that way with the drink.'

Spike bought the cigarettes and received some words of wisdom in Chinese from the shop keeper along with his change. Spike couldn't understand what was being said but he thanked the man anyway. *Ah so,* he replied, bowing his head, before joining the others who were heading back to the pub. The snow was falling heavily by now, blowing in their faces and making them reach for the buttons on their jackets. Spike was taking up the rear, muttering in his new found language. They were freezing cold by the time they reached The Prince Albert. Harry and Podger brushed most of the snow away and were first through the door. Spike didn't bother. He wandered in looking like a mobile igloo, causing the conversation in the bar to stop.

'What are you all looking at? Any chance of a whisky?'

'Bloody hell, it's a talking snowman that drinks whisky. Whatever next?' was uttered from the girls at the table.

'Is that you under there, Spike?' asked Alex.

'Course it's me. Who do you think it is? Get me a drink. I'm bloody freezing!'

'Will you be wanting some ice in it, Spike? Or are you just going to jump in the glass.' Spike was starting to thaw out with the heat of the public bar. A pool of water was forming at his feet.

'Oh, look! The poor snowman has wet himself. It must be the custom in Greenland just to do it on the floor,' laughed Alex. 'Welcome to our country, Mr Snowman. Would you care to join us for a drink? But first we should point out that we have a long standing tradition here in Scotland regarding the use of the toilets. We go to these little cubicles to do our business. We don't just piss where we're standing!' The crowd in the bar was enjoying this send up of Spike.

'Very funny! You buggers move over and let me sit down.' Spike had sobered up quite a bit since his return from his errand outside and was now almost back to normal. The girls were not finished with him yet.

'Tell us, Mr Snowman, do you know Santa Claus? He must be one of your neighbours.'

'*Ah so*, we hang out now and again. I sometimes borrow Rudolf for the ploughing.'

'Oh, and what do you grow?'

'Tomatoes, cucumbers and peppers. All of those things. Exotic fruit as well.'

'Isn't it a bit cold for those crops?'

'No, no, we have a wonderful climate up there. We sunbathe for most of the year in between growing the grapes. All that snow that you see? We import it just for the tourists. I'll probably take a few bags of your snow home with me when I go back. It looks to be fairly good quality. We're fussy, you know. Fancy rubbing noses? What time is Gerry closing tonight?'

'He's staying open till eleven o'clock. Let's all put some more money in the kitty. Wendy and I will go and get us more drinks,' said Alex.

The money in the ashtray was topped up and it was confirmed that closing time was to be eleven. By the time the hour arrived the crowd in the bar were in high spirits, singing and shouting with Vince and his chums leading the rabble. Gerry called time and was doing his best to get rid of the drunks. He was eager to get home in time for the midnight bells to herald the New Year. It was nearly half-past eleven before he managed to close the door on

Spike, who was the last one to leave.

'Goodnight, Spike. Have a good one. See you soon.'

'And goodnight to you, Gerry, and thanks for your *hostility.*'

It was still snowing as they stumbled and staggered down the street. There was hardly any traffic to be seen apart from the buses that were running every half-hour, taking passengers to whatever far-flung part of town was their choice. The council had decided to do what they had done in previous years and run the bus service free for the late night revellers.

'We'd better decide where we're going. It's ten to twelve,' said a none too sober Vince.

Wendy and Alex were on either side of Harry, supporting each other from falling down as they trudged through the snow. Podger and Spike were ahead of the rest, chucking snowballs at anything that moved. They had a particular fondness for the town buses which were getting pelted as they passed, heading in different directions. Not every shot was a hit. It was proving quite difficult to maintain any balance on the icy surface. Most of them made a visit to the ground at some place along the route. By the time the big clock in the square had chimed the start of the New Year they had travelled about a hundred yards in total. They were trying to get to the bus stop that would take them to the part of town where Wilf stayed. It was unanimous that it was as good a choice as any.

'Happy New Year!' they were shouting as they thrashed about in the snow. Trying to stay on their feet long enough to embrace one another was proving to be an impossible task. They met up in one big pile on the pavement just as the clock finished striking.

'We'd better open the bottles and have a celebration drink.'

'Good idea. Did anyone bring the glasses?'

'Bugger, I knew there was something we should have stolen. Never mind, just take a swig from the bottle.'

The bottles of whisky and vodka were fished out of the carrier bags and passed around with the usual face pulling as they drank the neat liquid.

'Yuk! That's strong!' spat Wendy. 'Have we something to pour it into?'

'We could drink some of the bottle then we'd have room for a mixer.' Alex and Wendy managed to get a quarter of the bottle of vodka drunk and then mixed in the lemonade. The lads were doing just fine drinking the neat whisky. They had almost finished one of the bottles with Spike getting more than his fair share. They stumbled along, finally reaching the stop for the number nine. They only had to wait a few minutes before the bus came into view through the swirling snow.

'Is this the bus that goes past Ramsay Street?' Vince had to ask the driver when the door opened. The sign above was obscured by the bad weather. It was doubtful if they could have read it anyway due to the inebriated state they were in. The driver nodded and they all piled in to join the other travellers. The bus was half full with an elderly chap trying to play the harmonica above the noise of a party, who were trying to sing Christmas songs. The driver could be seen looking in the mirror, shaking his head and thinking, 'Christ! I'm on until four!' It seemed a shame to get off when the call for Ramsay Street came. The gang were just getting into the swing of things, having had a few more swigs from the carry-out. When the door opened they fell out on to the pavement. Considering the state they were in, any other method of getting off would have been out of the question.

'Where are we going, Odd Job?'

'To see Wilf. He stays round the corner.'

'A corner!' someone shouted. 'We're expected to negotiate a corner!'

'Is there any chance I could spend less time on my arse!' Harry shouted from ground level.

'Come on, follow me, you lot. Get up will you.' Vince shouted over his shoulder as he made his way into the dark cul-de-sac.

'Can't you tell Wilf to come out here? None of our legs are working.'

'Or better still, give us a push!' They managed somehow, yet again, to get to the upright position.

'Odd Job, where are you? Don't leave us here!'

'Well, hurry up then,' said the voice from the darkness. 'I'm over here!' They staggered in a line to where the sound had come from and were doing quite well until Spike bumped into a lamp post, bringing himself down along with Wendy who was hanging on to his jacket.

'For fuck's sake! Are we ever going to get there? I could have reached the North Pole by now and claimed it for my country. Let's set up base camp here. I'm pooped,' said Spike, lighting a cigarette.

Alex was on her feet once more to see if she could

locate Vince. 'My prince, are you there? Can you send for Tonto or Skippy? We're having a helluva problem with this walking thing!'

'We've arrived, come on.' Vince appeared out of the darkness and put his arms around Alex to lend support.

'Thank goodness I've found you, my prince,' she gasped, giving him his first real kiss of the year.

'Where are the others? Hoi, you lot, over here. Where are they? I thought they were with you, Alex.'

'They've all perished in the snow, frozen to the pavement. We'll probably find their bodies when the snow melts in March. Never mind, I've held on to one of the carrier bags. Spike's got the other. Poor Spike, we'll all miss him...and the others.'

'We're here! We're here!' Spike and the others had caught up. 'I had an argument with a lamp post. The bloody thing jumped out and bushwhacked me. My ciggie's not lit. It's all wet.'

'That's not surprising. Look, you've cut your finger...it's covered in blood.'

'Thank goodness for that, I thought it was whisky.'

Vince rang the bell. Wilf opened the door with a glass in his hand. 'Vinz, yez came, come in, Charlez's here.'

'I've brought some mates. Do you mind?'

'No, bring them in. Whez are thez?

'They're crawling about in your front garden. We're all a bit pissed.'

'Wez pizzed az well. Come and meet the mizzuz.'

Harry was relieving himself in a dark corner of the garden when it came bounding through the door. It shot past Wilf and Vince and leaped on to Harry, knocking him over and into a snow-drift which was growing by the minute.

'Gez back in hez yez mutt!' Wilf shouted in vain. He'd had an Irish wolfhound as a pet ever since it had been bought as a puppy. Vince looked at it and thought, 'That thing wouldn't look out of place under starters orders in the two-thirty at Doncaster.' Podger, Alex and Wendy finally made it to the door along with Spike.

'Where's Harry?'

'I'm in here!' said a faint voice from the garden. Wilf's dog was sitting on top of the snowdrift that covered their chum. 'Get me out, will you!'

'Holy shit, where did the horse come from?'

'Help me out of here!'

'Harry, is that you?'

'Yes, of course it's me!'

'Bloody hell, he's been eaten by a monster!' Wilf switched on the outside light to get a better view. His dog was sitting on top of the pile of snow with a look of satisfaction, having foiled the intruder who'd dared piss in his garden.

'Gez back in the house, yez mutt. Come hez right now!'

The animal begrudgingly gave up its post and trundled over to its master, revealing a head and arm sticking out of the snowy tomb.

'Harry, are you alright. What are you doing in there?'

'I'm picking strawberries! What the fuck do you think I'm doing? Has that thing gone?'

Wendy and Alex couldn't get up off the snowy ground. They had fallen down with laughter at the sight of

Harry wearing a snowsuit. 'Can't we stick a red nose on him and just leave him there? He looks quite fetching.'

'Better not, he'll scare the birds.'

Harry was dug out and dusted down. Not long after, they were all in the house in front of the fire with a drink in their hand.

'Happy New Year, everyone.' Wilf had introduced his wife who could just be seen making the sandwiches through the steamy mist that was rising from the clothes belonging to the sorry bunch of drunks.

'Have you been home yet, Charlie?' asked Vince, addressing the figure slouched in the armchair.

'Nope, haven't quite made it that far. Wilf and me went for a drink after work and we ended up back here just before it started snowing heavily. I've phoned the wife. She's not bothered. Her sister's staying with us. She came up for Christmas so the two of them will be having a good old natter as usual.'

In addition to Wilf's talent of speaking and whistling simultaneously, he was also blessed with a surname that was quite a mouthful especially if you'd had a few drinks. Spike's attempts at conversation with Jenny McLusky had to be modified slightly.

'Can I call you Mrs Wilf?'

'Please yourself. Jenny will do,' she replied, handing round the side plates. She had been called worse names before. The bottles were passed round again. Wendy fell asleep on the sofa alongside Podger. The others were hanging on. The heat from the coal fire, combined with the alcohol they'd consumed, was making Alex yawn. She had her head on Vince's shoulder.

'Are you OK?' he whispered.

'Yes, my prince. I'm just a little sleepy. Do you mind if I do not ravish you tonight? I've been on my feet all day. Well, half the day. I've been on my arse quite a bit as well.' She started to get the giggles as she thought about their night's adventure. Mrs Wilf handed round a huge plate of sandwiches and sausage rolls, encouraging everyone to get stuck in. She left a plateful each for Wendy and Podger in case they should wake up feeling hungry.

'Why is the dog giving me that funny look? I thought we were friends now,' asked Harry.

'It's probably because you have its plate!'

The night wore on with less and less drink being consumed, plenty of meaningless talk and the odd sandwich and cups of tea appearing at sporadic intervals. Someone poked their head out of the front door to check on the weather and came back with the announcement, 'We're snowed in good and proper!' Harry had fallen asleep with his head resting on the Irish wolfhound, after having his face licked several times. The girls were all asleep apart from Mrs Wilf. She seemed to be blessed with boundless energy, washing glasses quicker than the others could dirty them. Podger was still asleep dreaming of some far off bicycle shed. Spike had lasted remarkably well considering the amount of alcohol he had poured over his throat. He was in mid-sentence, talking to Wilf and Charlie, when he ran out of steam. He placed his drink carefully on the sideboard, muttered, *Ah so*, and passed out, sliding to the floor gracefully in a way that was totally out of character for him. It wasn't long before

Vince succumbed to the heat of the roaring fire. Mrs Wilf persuaded her husband to go to his bed. Charlie was sent to the spare room. Podger who had been sleeping the longest, woke up after five in the morning ready for action but on seeing the lifeless bodies strewn before him, went back to sleep after he paid a visit to Wilf's toilet. It would be quite some time that morning before they would get themselves sorted out and they hadn't even been home yet.

'A Happy New Year!' Spike woke up ready for action, holding a bottle of beer with which to quench his thirst. The effects of last night's drinking spree had not worn off entirely. It would only take a few drinks to be back up to capacity.

'For Christ's sake, Spike, go back to sleep!' Vince and Alex had been entwined together, sleeping. They had been rudely awakened by the person that stood before them.

'Sleep! We've finished sleeping. It's party time. Get up you lazy shites!'

The other bodies on the floor were starting to stir to the groans of, 'Oh my bloody head.'

'Have another drink, your headache will disappear.'

'Is there any chance that you'll disappear too?'

'Now, now, Harry, where's your girlfriend. Been stood up?' said Spike, referring to the absence of Wilf's dog.

'Where are we anyway?' mumbled Podger. He and Wendy were the brightest, having had the most sleep. 'Christ!' said Podger, looking at the person lying beside him. 'I've slept with the minister's daughter. I'm going to get some mileage out of this story.'

'You try and I'll tell everyone that you're hopeless.'

'Just kidding, Wendy, incidentally, how was it for you?'

Wendy threw a cushion at Podger just as Mrs McLuskey came into the room. Spike was the first to speak.

'*Ah so*. Good morning, Mrs Wilf, and a Happy New Year to you.'

'It's Jenny!'

'Sorry, Mrs Jenny, and where is your spouse this fine day?'

'He's still sleeping it off. Charlie's not surfaced either. Are any of you wanting breakfast?'

The bleary-eyed bunch looked at the table set with forks and knives. A very large teapot was pride of place, the steam from its spout indicating that the tea had been newly made. The room was tidy without a trace of the previous night's drinking session.

'Goodness, Mrs McLuskey, I mean, Jenny. How on earth do you manage it? Aren't you tired, have you had any sleep?' asked Alex.

'I've had a couple of hours...plenty for me. Now who's wanting bacon and eggs?'

'You've been cooking as well?' asked an equally impressed Wendy.

'Sit yourselves down, there's toast on the table. Come on now, you can't be going out drinking on an empty stomach.' Jenny ushered them to the table and was off and into the kitchen, emerging with a huge plate of bacon in one hand and a plate of eggs in the other.

'Where's all the booze?' inquired Spike, dreading the

thought that they might be stranded without any.

'I've put your bottles over there...or what's left of them.' Jenny pointed to the row of nearly empty bottles all lined up in perfect formation.

'*Ah so.*' They had just started eating when Charlie and Wilf appeared rather the worse for wear.

'Hello, howz yez all?'

'A Happy NewYear to you both. This is very good of you and Mrs Jenny to provide us with these victuals for our onward journey. What time do you want us back for supper?' piped up Spike again.

Wilf looked out from under his bleary eyes and thought, 'Oh, it's the mad one! Yez moz welcome, Spike. Howz are yez girlz?'

'We're fine, Wilf. Thank you for having us. Where is your horse...I mean, dog?'

'The mutz outside somewhez, probably having a shitz.' As if on cue, the gigantic beast came bounding through the half-open door and jumped on Harry, knocking him off his chair and pinning him to the floor.

'My dog likes yez.'

'Your girlfriend's back, Harry.'

'Listen you lot, we'll have to get home soon and see our folks and Norman as well. Have you any suggestions, my prince?' asked Alex.

'I know that there's a special bus service at ten. I think it only runs the one time. What time is it?'

'Quarter to ten.'

'Bloody hell, let's get a move on or we'll miss it. Thanks again for everything, Jenny. You too, Wilf. Come on you lot, get on your feet.'

They quickly grabbed the bottles along with their dry clothes. It took them ten minutes to reach the bus stop. They were a bit more sure-footed this time. It helped that the snow had stopped and the roads had been gritted.

'I see that our lads have been earning some overtime,' said Vince.

'Can I have some as well, my prince. Have you seen Tonto to wish him a Happy New Year? I suppose he'll be lying at the foot of some totem pole out of his head on firewater.'

They had the entire bus to themselves as they made their way to Berrydale, which was just as well considering the noise they were making. They had almost emptied all the bottles by the time they reached the village. As soon as they were off the bus they started a snowball fight and then it was decision time.

'Where are we going first?'

'Let's go and see Norman and his folks.'

Mrs Halford answered the door to be greeted by the rabble in front of her.

'I was wondering where you lot had got to. Come on in.'

'Where's Norman then? We need to give him a hug,' asked Alex, feeling the effect of the now empty bottle of vodka.

'Norman! Are you up yet?' shouted Mr Halford who'd joined them in the lounge. 'Your mates are here. We had a few people round last night. Pamela and Matthew were here along with your Dad, Wendy.'

'And how is my pops? Has he disowned me yet?'

'He knew you were with your mates. He wasn't that

concerned about you.'

'Norman! A Happy New Year to you.' The sleepy head had appeared wearing a big grin.

'How are you all? Have you had a good time?'

'We've been to Wilf's. We missed not having you with us,' replied Wendy, giving him a big hug. The others followed, taking it in turn to wish their chum all the best for the coming year.

'I see you're trashed. I need to catch up.'

'Here you are,' said Podger, draining the last of the whisky from the bottle into a glass. 'We're running low on provisions.'

'Cheers, everyone.' Mr Halford poured out a drink for the rest of them and they were soon settled down for another session. Someone had mentioned they would have to go and find more bottles. The idea was soon forgotten about as they proceeded to empty the contents of the Halford's drinks' cabinet. It was late in the day when they finally staggered home, after visiting a few more houses. Norman went along with them and he was soon as merry as the rest of them. Alex had phoned her folks to wish them a Happy New Year and to tell them where she was. They dropped in past Wendy's first. They were there to lend moral support should she feel the wrath of her father. They need not have been concerned because the minister was in fine form, helped by all the gin and tonic he had consumed. They finally made it to Vince's house where they spent the remainder of the day and evening with Alex staying over, sleeping in Grandma's room. Harry fell asleep alongside Spike. They were snoring out loud and oblivious to the antics of Alex who had found some crayons and was making up Spike's face to resemble a dog.

'There, Harry will feel more at home now when he wakes up,' she said. 'You don't suppose Spike has fleas, do you?'

Norman and Podger were deep in conversation. 'Are you seeing anyone at the moment, Podge?'

'Nobody in particular. Why, do you fancy me?'

'No, not really, but I'll tell you what, I'll keep you high on my list.' They both laughed at the incredulity of the very idea.

'Anyway, I slept with the minister's daughter last night.'

'And how was it?'

'It was a very moving, religious experience.'

'Why, did she thump you with a bible?'

*

It so happened that Vince's twenty-first landed on a Friday. They had all arranged to go to town for the big occasion. Unknown to Vince, Spike had arranged for a stripper to be at The Prince Albert. He'd phoned the agency the week before asking the price. 'Can you make sure that I get a nice, pretty girl? It's for someone special.'

'We have just the girl for you. Claudia is her name. She will strip to her G-string that's all, no other nonsense. It'll be ten pounds cash. Pay her when she arrives.' Spike gave the details over the phone and arranged for her to be at The Prince Albert at nine o'clock. It was half-past seven when they arrived at the pub. The green room was used for private parties. Not too large, it was perfect for the twenty or so people that Vince had invited. It was not a formal invitation, more of a 'drop in if you're passing'. They could drink in the lounge and use the green room to get some of the food which had been organised.

'Right, are we all on pints?'

'Sounds good.'

'Three pints of lager, three whiskies please, Gerry.'

'What's the occasion tonight, lads? As if you need an excuse,' asked Woody who was propping up the bar on his usual stool.

'Odd Job's twenty-first.'

'Happy birthday, Vince.'

'Thanks, Woody, you'll be having a drink?'

'Wouldn't say no.'

'The food is all set out for you through the house, Vince. Just help yourself. You can square up with me later,' said Gerry as he poured the drinks.

'Thanks, there'll be some others coming in past. You know most of them. If you need us, just shout for Spike, Podge or me.'

Spike was already at work with a rather well-endowed female at the bar. 'What's your name?'

'Melanie.'

'How appropriate,' he thought.

'What's yours?'

'Spike, can I buy you a drink?'

'Bacardi and Coke, please.'

'Coming right up.'

The bar was quickly filling up with a lot of familiar faces dropping in past. Alex arrived, grabbed Vince's hand and led him away to the cupboard that held the empty beer bottles. She was determined to wish him a happy birthday before the evening got out of hand. Spike was well drunk by now. He'd had the elbow from the large breasted Melanie and was now eyeing up another girl who was deep in conversation with her friend.

'Hi, baby,' he slurred.

'Fuck off! You're stupid!'

'And you're ugly! Given the choice, I'd rather be stupid!' He shuffled over to where Vince and Podger were. Podger seemed to be doing better.

'And why are you called Podger?' inquired the nymph-like creature. 'You're not fat, you're rather cute.'

'You should have seen him when he was younger,' said Vince. 'He was a right little porker.'

'What's your proper name, then?'

'It's Robert actually, but I'm used to being called Podger.'

'Well, I'm going to call you Robbie. Will I see you later?'

'Maybe.'

Spike looked at his watch. It was nine o'clock. 'I'm off to the bog,' he said. He reached the front door just in time to see the stripper arrive wrapped in a trench coat.

'Are you the stripper?'

'Yes.' She turned round startled. 'Spike!'

'Lucy! For goodness sake! What are you doing here?'

'I'm with the agency. They told me to be here at nine. They said I had to meet someone called Ralph. I never twigged it would be you. Who's birthday is it anyway?'

'Odd Job's.'

'What! For Christ's sake!'

'But the agency said we would be getting Claudia?'

'That's my stage name,' she giggled.

'This is great, bloody great, here's the money. Give me two minutes and I'll get them all through to the green room. It's through there.' Spike was pointing to the door.

'I know where it is. I've been here before.'

'Odd Job!' Spike shouted. 'We could use some food.

'Just help yourself.'

'No, you have to come through. You're needed.'

'Alright, alright, I'm coming.'

They had just started to tuck in to the food on the table when they heard the music from the stripper's portable cassette: *Boom, boom, boom*. And then she appeared in her French maid's outfit. Vince's jaw dropped when he saw who it was. 'It's Lucy! Brilliant!'

Podger, who had been engaged in conversation with his new found friend, stopped in mid-sentence and gasped, 'Lucy!'

Boom, boom, boom. She took off her apron, then her boots. *Boom, boom, boom*. 'Get em off!' the crowd shouted. She was now down to her bra and G-string. *Boom, boom, boom*. Then it was all over with everyone clapping and cheering. She gave the victim a hug. 'How are you, Odd Job?'

'Great, who set this up?'

'Spike, I didn't know it was for you. My agency sent me,' she replied, gathering up her clothes.

'You do this for a living, now?'

'No, only part-time. I started doing it to help with the college fees and I've just carried on. The money's handy.'

'And you did it tonight, for nothing?'

'No bloody way, I've been paid.'

'Are you staying for a drink?'

'Yeah, OK, I suppose I could. This was my last gig tonight. Why isn't Podge here?'

'He is.'

'Where?'

'Over there,' replied Vince, pointing over to the corner.

Lucy looked over and saw the familiar features of a very handsome man. He walked over. 'Hello Lucy,' said Podger, giving her a hug.

'Podge! Is it really you?' she asked this desirable hunk.

'Yup.'

'You've lost so much weight. You look great.' He almost blushed but now he was a confident, young man.

'How long have you been doing this?'

'For a while now. It's only part-time. It's all above board...I don't go as far as some of them do,' she said quickly.

'I know, I know.'

'Come on, let's all have a drink. Gerry, set them up!' Spike shouted.

'Podge, do you fancy going back to my flat for a coffee? The other girls I share with are out tonight. It's not far. We can get a taxi.' It felt strange calling him that name now. It didn't seem appropriate.

'Yes, I'd like that. I'll tell the others.'

'Another round!' someone shouted.

'Listen, guys, I'm going to make my own way back tonight. I'll catch up with you later.'

'Oooh, love is in the air,' they crooned in harmony.

'Give us a break, please. I'll see you tomorrow.'

'Are you going to be alright?'

'I'll be fine, Odd Job. I'm waiting for Lucy. She's getting changed.'

'You be a good boy now.'

They set off after goodnight hugs and the usual whistling. Lucy and Podger hailed a cab and twenty minutes later they were settled in her flat.

'Sorry about the mess. I left in a hurry,' she said, picking up the underwear that was strewn about the room.

'That's OK, I've kind of got used to seeing your knickers over the years.'

'You look fabulous, Podge. How did you manage to lose so much weight?' she asked, handing him the coffee.

'I run most days and I watch what I eat. The weight just seems to fall off.' He didn't venture to tell her that she was his inspiration after the encounter in her house all those years ago.

'Can I start calling you Bob?'

'Robbie would be better.'

'I've thought about you a lot.'

'Me too, Lucy.'

'You didn't mind the show then? I left on my top and bottom.'

'No,' he lied.

'Just because I strip part-time doesn't mean I'm an easy girl. I don't want you thinking...'

'It's OK,' he said, interrupting. 'I know you're not like that. You're just a show-off really,' he said, gazing into her eyes.

'I can't believe it's really you. You're so different. It's ages since I've seen you, or seen any of you, apart from Wendy and Alex. She's bloody mental, isn't she? But great fun.'

'Who, Wendy?'

'No, Double Sandy. She adores Odd Job but tries not to show it too much.'

'Yeah, I know. He's pretty fond of her as well.'

'Do you think they'll get married?'

'Who knows with those two? They're both bloody crazy. How's work with you? I hear that you're doing alright with that firm. Do they not mind you taking your clothes off?'

'I try and keep them on in the office. Well actually, I haven't told them. I keep saying I'll stop before they find out. It's fun and anyway, there's the money I get.'

'Well, I'm sure you know best.'

'Norman's pretty ill, isn't he?'

'Yes, but we're all hoping he'll be drawing his old age pension with the rest of us.'

'What about Spike? Just about every girl I meet seems to have been out with him and his Zephyr.'

'I know. If he'd been a woman, he'd be called a right tart.'

'And Harry?'

'He's doing OK. He's making good money.'

'Is Rosemary still at school?'

'Ah, Runny Nose. I think she finishes this year. She's quite popular with the boys as well. Do you have a boyfriend, Lucy?'

'No.' She wanted so much to grab him in her arms. 'I

haven't that much time for boys. I'm too busy with work. If I had, would you be jealous?' she said with a laugh.

'Maybe, just a bit.'

'What about you? I'll bet all the girls are chasing you, yeah?'

'I should be so lucky. I keep thinking about you. Is that silly?'

'Oh, Podge...I mean Robbie. I think about you a lot as well. Do you remember that night in my house? Was I awful and cheap?'

'I don't remember what you charged. You certainly weren't awful.'

'You know what I mean,' she said, giving him a playful slap.

'No, it's OK. I know you were feeling sorry for me, Lucy.' He moved to touch her.

'Shh, wait here.' She went through to her bedroom and came back with her cassette player. Lucy pressed the play button: *Boom, boom, boom.* Her dance was different...special, sexier. She writhed in front of him, slowly peeling off her clothes. She remembered their last meeting. *Boom, boom, boom.* She was flushed. She took off her top and let him touch her breasts which were fuller now. She was excited. She didn't want to stop. *Boom, boom, boom.* He caressed her. He was excited. He didn't want her to stop. 'Don't stop, don't stop,' he cried. *Boom, boom, boom.* She flicked her G-string off and leaned onto him. They shared a long and meaningful kiss.

'Do you want to go to the bedroom?' she gasped.

'Nah, I'd rather stay here with you.'

They laughed. It was always meant to be.

Chapter Thirteen
1976-1977. Norman's Illness.

Norman's condition had been getting worse. He had not been well enough to go to his work for some time. The management of *The Spokesman* had been sympathetic to his illness. They had been supportive over the weeks and months, allowing him time off when he wasn't well enough to attend his work. It was a mutual decision that he should leave the company.

The whole community was devastated by the news of Norman's leukaemia. He had been on medication for some time now. The Halfords had originally been told that his condition might remain stable for many years but now, after further tests, they were informed that his illness was a particularly nasty variant. Norman had been picking up more and more infections and he suffered from terrible tiredness. When Norman's friends were first told of his condition they assumed that he would be around for as long as them. Vince had asked Wendy to have a word with the consultant as to what the prognosis was to be. She came back with the answer that Norman's illness could be treated and he could lead a normal life. This good news was distributed by Vince to all of Norman's friends and it was decided that they would torment

Norman the same as they always had. He was a cheeky hooligan just like the rest of them. Vince and the others would take every opportunity to call in past his house and drag him off on some mischievous mission. 'Come on you lazy bugger, we're going to town for some fun.' Norman was an eager participant in these activities. He would be the first one in the car, usually riding up front. Norman would arrive back home invigorated by his evening with the others and would still be laughing as he threw his jacket on the cake-stand on his way upstairs to bed.

*

Spike had his eye on another car. The Zephyr had been a trusty motor but now it was getting a bit old and rusty. He fancied a change and the Ford Capri that was sitting in the dealer's yard in town was just what he wanted. He reasoned that it would do him until he could afford the Jag. Vince and Harry agreed to go along with him to make sure he was getting a good deal. It was as good an excuse as any to go into town.

'There it is.'

'Where?'

'Over there.' Spike was pointing to the car that was parked behind the newer models on display. 'Nice, eh? Sixteen hundred GT. Does a hundred miles an hour.'

'That's no use to you, Spike. You've never been away from the girls for longer than ten minutes. How are you going to manage an hour? Can't you get a new one? This thing must be a few years old.'

'I'm going to see what I'll get for my Zephyr.' Spike wandered off and into the showroom. He had spoken to the salesman before and knew the price. There was just the small matter of his Zephyr to be negotiated. The salesman looked over his car and offered him fifty pounds trade-in. He said it was the best that he could do despite Spike's claims that it was a girl magnet. Spike could hardly wait to get behind the wheel of the Capri. He'd already had a test drive the day before. The deal was done and the three of them set off back to Berrydale.

'No sliding seat in this one, Spike. Bit of a disappointment,' said Vince.

'Don't need one. This is just the dog's bollocks, isn't it?'

'Do you think that Elvis will like it?' asked Harry.

'Probably, he's got a good eye for cars. He'll have one of these in his fleet next to his Cadillac. What do you think, Odd Job?'

'Uh huh,' replied Vince, curling his lip.

Chapter Fourteen
1977-1979. The Wedding.

'Will you manage to go to the wedding, Norman?'

'I'll be there, Odd Job.'

Podger had announced that he and Lucy were to get married. They had been seeing each other for quite some time and everyone agreed that it was a good match. They'd asked Vince if he'd be best man and he was delighted to accept.

'I'll probably just go to the reception. If I'm there the whole day I'll not last the pace, trying to keep up with you lot.'

'Since when have you had a problem keeping up?' asked Vince.

'Well, you know.'

'Yeah, I know. Just make sure you're there or we'll come and drag you out of the house.'

'I wouldn't miss it for the world. Funny isn't it?' said Norman.

'What?'

'Podge and Lucy getting together. Every time I see him I can hardly believe it, he was such a fat bugger.'

'Yeah, he's probably put some pie making factory out

of business since he's gone all slim.'

'What's the matter, Spike? You look as if you've lost the map showing the way to the girls.' He had arrived to check on Norman.

'Did you hear about Elvis?'

'Is he coming over to visit you at last, Spike.'

'He's dead!'

'Dead?'

'Yeah.'

'What do you mean? Dead as in not being alive?'

'Didn't you hear it on the news?'

'No,' said Vince. He could see that Spike was really upset. The news was quite a shock to Vince as well. He was an admirer of the King, along with millions of others.

'Christ! That's hard to imagine. I thought he'd go on forever,' said Norman, equally surprised.

'I know, so did I,' replied Spike with a sigh.

'You were going to go and see him in Las Vegas as well, weren't you?' In the past, they had spoken about the possibility of going to America but as with most dreams, converting them into reality was a different thing altogether.

'Elvis dead,' Spike said again, shaking his head. 'I'm off to see if there's any more news on the TV.' He headed off in the direction of his house and waved to Harry on the way.

'Spike's heard the news, then?' asked Harry.

'Yeah, we've just been talking about it.'

'Is he going to the funeral?'

'It's not funny. The King's dead, for fuck's sake.'

'Yeah, I know, it's sad. Are we all set for this wedding

then?'

'I'm looking forward to it. I thought we could all chip in some money rather than give them a present.'

'Odd Job's right. It won't stop them ending up with two toasters or four bloody irons but at least they won't be from us.'

'Yeah, good thinking.'

*

It was a fine day for the wedding. The sun was shining, the birds were singing, the victims were nervous. Vince and Spike arranged to pick up Podger at twelve o'clock. The service was to start at two but they needed a drink to calm their nerves. Mr Chalmers answered the door. 'Hello, lads, Robert's almost ready. I don't know who's the worst, him or the missus. Robert, are you ready? The lads are here for you.'

'Coming,' he appeared at the door with his Mum.

'Now listen, don't go drinking too much. I know what you lot are like when you get together. This is a special day so don't spoil it.'

'Yes, Mrs Chalmers,' was the uniform reply.

'And don't be late,' she continued. 'You just have the one drink now, you hear?'

'Don't worry. We'll be there on time.'

'Have you got the ring, Vincent?'

'Yes, Mrs Chalmers. It's in my pocket. Look here it is,' said Vince over his shoulder as he headed with the other two for Spike's Capri.

'Three pints, George.'

'Are you all set then, Robert? It's a big day for you.'

'It'll be a piece of cake, George. Odd Job...have you

got the ring?'

'Yes, Podge.'

'Show us.'

'Oh, for Christ's sake, calm down. George, give us three whiskies please.'

'Coming up, Spike.'

Victoria was cleaning the tables beside the dart board, leaning over with her back to them. They could just see the white of her panties. Spike was drooling. 'There's something in there that all men want.'

'What, a pint of lager? How does she manage to fit that in there Spike? Why don't you just ask her out?'

'Ask who out?' George was back from sorting the beer pipes.

'It's Spike. He fancies your daughter.'

'You leave my girl alone. She's saving herself for someone special. Victoria! Stop flashing your knickers. You're getting these lads excited.'

'I'm surprised at you, Podge. You're about to get married'

'It's not me, Victoria, it's Spike. He's got the hots for you. Are you coming to the reception later?'

'I'll try, depends how busy Dad's going to be tonight.'

'You go ahead, girl. We'll be pretty quiet I should think. Most of our regulars will be at the wedding. Here, lads, get this down you. Have a drink on me. Here's to the condemned man.'

'Cheers, George.'

'By the way, is Norman going to the wedding?'

'He'll be there. He's doing OK. He gets a bit tired now and again. He's fine...,' said an unconvincing Vince.

'Get's another round, George.'

'Slow down, Odd Job, we'll all be pissed.'

'Stop worrying, Podge, it's not every day you get married. We've plenty of time, just relax. I'm going to the toilet. Spike, get them in.'

'Who's that girl Harry's seeing? She looks as if she fell out of the ugly tree.'

'She's from somewhere in town. C'mon, she's not that bad.'

'Maybe I saw her in a bad light. We'll get a closer look tonight. She'll be at the reception, won't she?'

'Probably, he'll be showing her off.'

Vince arrived back. 'Who are you talking about?'

'Harry's bird. Have you seen her, Odd Job?'

'Yup, she's OK.'

'Spike thinks she's bow wow city. He thinks they should all look like Victoria. Harry seems pleased enough, says she goes like a rabbit. Is Double Sandy coming to the reception?'

'She's been asked. She likes all that weepy stuff.'

'George, are you there?'

'Just a minute, Spike. Same again is it?'

'Yeah, and have you got any carrots?'

'Carrots!'

'Yeah, carrots, you know? Them orangey-red things that you get in soup.'

'I know what they look like. I've chopped enough the bloody things. I've got some in the kitchen f' weekend. What are you up to now?'

'Can you give us a bunch?'

'I suppose so. Who's on the receiving ℯ

Spike looked around to make sure that Victoria wasn't listening. 'Harry says that his new girlfriend goes like a rabbit. So go on, lend me some.'

'Alright, don't say that you got them from me. Are you lads watching the time?'

'Christ! We're going to be late.'

'We've time for one more, Podge.'

'Not for me. Have you got the ring?'

'Yes, yes. Another two then, George.'

'Hurry up you three. You'll miss the wedding. I'll drive you to the church. You've had enough to drink.'

George shoved them into his Volvo and drove them and the bunch of carrots to the church.

'I need the toilet,' said Spike.

'You'll have to wait. We're almost there.'

There were a few anxious faces as they rolled out of the car. The Reverend Calder was pacing up and down along with Podger's Mum and Dad and a few others.

'Where have you been? The bride's already been round the village twice. Where's Robert and Spike off to now?'

'Sorry, Mrs Chalmers, terrible queue at the bar. They've just gone to the lav.' They had spotted the emergency toilet to the left of the graveyard, grateful that yew trees and churches went together.

'You're pissing on my leg!'

'Well, move over a bit.'

'Bugger off, the bridesmaids are looking.'

'Hurry up, you two. Get in the church, the bride's rriving.'

'What's Spike doing with those carrots, Vincent?'

'Dunno, Mrs Chalmers. I think he's making soup later.'

Somehow they managed to get into the church and find their places just as the bride arrived at the gate. Vince sat down on the front pew to gather his thoughts for this important occasion. He wished he hadn't had that last drink at the bar. The organ was playing and he found himself counting the missed notes.

'Dee deet de de...dah de dah...oops!'

'Do you, Podger, who was once a fat bastard but you sorted that and are now a handsome prince...take this stripper who likes to show off her knickers behind the shed that holds the bikes...to be your lawful wed...?'

'Vincent! Vincent, wake up!' It was the minister poking him on the arm. 'Would you care to join us?' Vince looked around sheepishly at the stern faces. Spike was sitting in the pew, creased with laughter and holding the bunch of carrots.

'Yes, of course, minister.' He looked at the bride... a vision of beauty in her lovely dress. He looked at the groom who was wearing a stupid grin and a wet stain on the front of his trousers. Vince stood up and took his place beside them.

'We are gathered here today...'

'Hic.'

'To join these...'

'Hic.'

Podger had contracted the disease feared by all at a time like this, the dreaded hiccups.

'Hold your breath, lad,' whispered the minister. 'Or we'll be here all day!'

Somehow Podger managed to get through the ceremony with the odd stifled noise. It did sound a bit strange towards the end when the congregation heard the reply to a question. 'I...hic...do.' It also was very unromantic when it came to the bit where the bride was kissed. Podger was having difficulty aiming for Lucy's lips with his whisky sodden mouth. The vows over, they all filed out of the church for the photographs. It was then that the photographer had the difficult task of trying to arrange the entourage for the photographs. Lucy was not amused as she witnessed a few more visits to the yew tree being made. She was glad when they finally set off for the Legion. Lucy and Podger were being driven in the Bentley, leaving the rest to make do with the bus. The Legion was prepared for the onslaught. The tables were ready. The cold buffet was set out. The band had already set up. Norman was there and he was the first to greet the happy couple.

'Norman, glad you could make it.'

'Congratulations, you two,' he said, giving them both a big hug.

'How are you?'

'I'm fine, really. I'm gonna get you two a drink. What are you having?'

'I'll have a glass of wine, please. I'm gagging.'

'Podge?'

'I could use a pint.'

'You go easy. You've already had a skin full. Can you believe this bugger...my new husband... he was in the pub with Spike and Odd Job. They got half-pissed and Odd Job fell asleep in the church. Then this one here got the hiccups. Christ, what an embarrassment.'

'Hey, Norman.' The bus had arrived. The bar was filling up.

'Somebody grab a table. That big one over there,' shouted Spike, pointing to the one that would give them a good view of the girls who had already claimed the table beside the food. They sat down with their drinks in front of them.

'What are you going to do with those carrots, Spike?'

'They're for Harry,' he replied, wrapping them in a large napkin he had found. 'Where is he anyway?'

'He's over there with his bird talking to Lucy. Are we putting in a kitty?'

'Good idea. Are you joining us, Harry?'

'Hello, everybody, this is Veronica. She'll know some of you already.'

'Hello,' she said. 'Will you excuse me for a moment? I'm going to the ladies.'

'Harry, what's she like?' Spike whispered.

'She's a bit of a goer,' he whispered back.

'I've heard that she goes like a rabbit.'

'Yeah.'

'Then, you'll be needing these,' said Spike, handing over the napkin and its contents.

'Oh, for Christ's sake!' laughed Harry.

'What's that?' Veronica had returned.

'Eh...nothing, just the lads playing a joke.'

'Well, let me in on it.'

'Somebody give me a hand at the bar with the drinks.' Vince quickly changed the subject.

'I'll give you a hand,' volunteered Norman.

'Hoi! Norman!' It was Spike. 'Round up some hostages.' He was still eyeing up the girls at the other table.

Wendy arrived with Alex. They had no trouble finding the table. It was the one with the most noise coming from it.

'Hello, everyone.'

'Another two drinks for the girls.'

'We're just going over to speak to Lucy and Podge. We'll be right back. Come on, Alex.'

Harry and Norman had to queue at the bar but eventually they came back with the drinks.

'Who's wanting these?' Norman asked, offering up the sausages speared with cocktail sticks.

'Oh, for Christ's sake!' said Spike as the laughing continued.

'What have I done now?'

'Nothing, Norman, nothing,' laughed Vince. 'The sausages are for me.'

The speeches and the cutting of the cake were done and they were all eager to get on with the dancing. Vince had to say his bit as best man and somehow he managed to fumble his way through it without the urge for a sleep. Since arriving from the church he had been pacing himself and he was happy that it was over and done with. Podger stood up to make his reply and thankfully avoided the hiccups. Lucy's father was the last to say something and finished off with the words, 'Thank you for being here. Let's get on with the dancing.' Vince arrived back at the table with the others just as the band started to play their first number. They had a country and western band called The Ho-Downs playing that night with a girl singer dressed like Dolly Parton and almost as big. The Reverend Calder stopped at the table to check on his daughter who was giggling along with the rest of the girls.

'Well, I think everything went quite well.' He had a glazed expression, the result of quite a few gins.

'Yes, minister. Can we get you a drink?'

'Maybe later, I must go and mingle.'

The girls were on the floor, dancing round their handbags. The men had more serious things to consider.

'We'll have to put more money in the kitty. We're running low. Come on, another fiver each.'

As soon as Lucy and Podger had changed, they were back handing out cake with the bridesmaids. The bridesmaids were two of Lucy's flat-mates. Wendy had been asked if she wanted to be a bridesmaid but she'd said she was a bit shy and would rather not. That had made it easier for Lucy to choose her chums from town, avoiding any squabbling.

'Get on your feet, Odd Job. I have to have a dance with the best man before you all get legless.'

'I'm your man, Lucy.'

'Come on Alex,' said Podger. 'We'll show them how it's done.'

The dance floor was now awash with arms, legs and handbags. They all had a different style of dancing to *Blanket on the Ground*. The Reverend Calder was getting stuck in, rendering a particularly artistic version that required very clever footwork on his part. The man of God was a person liked by all in the community. He was always to be seen at weddings and funerals and was good company should anyone bump into him on a New Year's Eve.

Earlier on that year, in the first week in January, the Reverend Calder had wandered up to Brodie's farm with Matthew for their New Year drink. Spike's Dad, Donald, was already there and they'd all had a drinking session lasting into the small hours. At three o'clock in the morning the three men set off for home. The walking surface was slippery due to the snow that had fallen on top of the frosty ground. They had managed to stay on their feet until they reached the grid that stopped Brodie's sheep from straying. They paused to have a drink from the bottle that Donald was still carrying when the Reverend slipped and fell rolling over into the bushes. It wasn't until he tried to speak that he realised he was minus the top set of his false teeth. After a brief search on the ground, it was agreed that they had little chance of finding his dentures in the darkness. The next day Vince was despatched by his father to find the missing teeth but seemingly to no avail. After much searching by the Reverend himself, he had to resign himself to preaching without them, much to the amusement of all, including Vince who had announced that he and Norman were to be part of the congregation that Sunday. The minister was relieved to get the shorter than normal service over with. He was even more relieved when Vince had gone back for another look for his false teeth and had miraculously discovered them on the ground.

'Thank you very much, Vincent. God works in mysterious ways.'

'He sure does, minister. He sure does.'

Spike was trying to impress one of the girls from the other table with his dancing. The girl was not amused. Spike had his shirt-tail hanging out and his sleeves rolled up. 'Hoi, Podge! How's married life?' he slurred.

'Great!' Podger shouted back. Lucy was trying to curtail Podger's drinking. She was thinking about the night ahead after the wedding reception was finished. Podger had many friends who all wanted to buy him a drink and wish him well. Spike was now dancing on his own. He hadn't noticed that his partner had left him to join her friends. It wasn't until the music stopped that he noticed she was gone. 'Where the hell is she?' he mumbled, just as Victoria arrived. 'Vikki, Vikki, Vikki, how about a dance?'

'Don't call me that, Spike...it's Victoria!'

'Oh, pardon me all over the place...Victoria!'

'Anyway, you're drunk. You can hardly stand.'

'OK, please yourself.' He turned round to Veronica. 'Can I have the pleasure, Veronica?'

Veronica, by now, was quite tipsy as well and Harry was not a dancer. 'Let's boogy,' she said.

The wedding reception was going well. Lorna and Micky spent most of the evening with Lucy's new mother and father-in-law. They and the Chalmers were getting on fine. The night came to an end with the last waltz, followed by a chorus of *He's a Jolly Good Fellow*. Spike had fallen asleep at the table. He'd had a busy night. He had given up on the girls. His last attempt had been with the busty singer who had thwarted his efforts. 'Hello, haven't you got nice boobies. Can I count them?'

She shook her head and walked away. She'd heard it

all before.

It was time to round up everyone for the bus. Lucy and Podger had arranged to stay the night at the Legion and then they would set off next day to go down south for a week. They didn't have a lot of money for a proper honeymoon. They wanted to use their savings for a house. Norman had already left with his Mum and Dad. He'd been feeling tired. It had been a long night for him.

'Hurry up, Spike! You'll miss the bus.'

'Go away and leave me here!' Vince and Harry had to walk him outside where he promptly threw up behind the coach.

'What, no carrots, Spike? Give us some carrots. We want carrots.'

'If you can find any, give 'em to Harry,' was the drunken reply.

Veronica was put in a taxi back to town. Alex had agreed to go with her to share the cost but not before Veronica managed to get to the ladies toilet just in time to throw up.

'When are we seeing each other again, Odd Job?'

'Dunno, Alex. I'll get in touch with you next week. We're all too drunk to do anything tonight.'

'I could manage,' she said, nibbling his ear.

'I know, I know. I have to get these drunken louts home. Besides, I'm knackered myself.'

The Reverend Calder was dragged off to the car by his wife, assisted by Wendy. They stuffed him in the front passenger side and he proceeded to have a deep and meaningful conversation with the dashboard. With all aboard the bus, the driver finally managed to get the door shut. He was instructed to drop them off at the post office back in the village. From there they would have to make their own way home. The driver was grateful that the journey only took ten minutes. A bus full of drunks, trying to sing four or five different songs was not his idea of entertainment. 'Still,' he thought, 'they're not as bad as those buggers from the rugby club that I had last week.'

*

Over the next few months Norman's condition became worse. He was now in bed for most of the time. His family and friends were regular visitors with the doctor calling in past whenever he could. The doctor had talked to the Halfords, preparing them for the inevitable. They kept a brave face in front of all who came past but the strain was beginning to show. One evening, when Vince arrived home from work, Pamela told him that Mrs Halford had phoned saying that Norman had asked for Vince and wanted him to go over to the house. The door was opened by a tired-looking mother who told Vince to go through to the bedroom.

'What is it, Norman?'

'I thought I'd get you over to annoy you, Odd Job. There's nothing good on the TV,' he whispered.

'Thanks, you bugger. I haven't had my supper yet.'

'Have you found the treasure?'

'No, I've given up on it just now. We'll have another look when you're feeling up to it.'

'Pity.'

'Do you want some of this water?' Vince was pointing to the glass on the bedside table.

'Naw, I could murder a pint, though.'

'I'll go and get you one.'

'No, no. I'm only joking,' he said with a smile.

'If you're wanting a pint, I'll get it for you right now.'

'No, really. I'm not thirsty, just sleepy.'

'Should I go now and let you sleep?'

'Are you wanting your supper?'

'No...I'm not hungry.'

'Stay a while longer. I'll kick your arse out the door when I've had enough of you.'

'Have you got everything you need? These grapes are rather tasty.'

'Grapes! I ordered olives. I thought they were a bit sweet.' Norman was struggling to keep his eyes open. 'I was dreaming earlier on about Patrick's pond. Remember the raft and the pram?'

'Have Lucy and Podge been in past recently?' Vince asked.

'Yeah, they were here a couple of days ago. She'll be having the baby soon, another bloody hooligan, no doubt.'

'Norman, you're tired. I'd better go and let you rest.'

'Yeah, thanks for coming round past.'

'It was your pleasure. I'll pop in past tomorrow. You get some rest.' Vince had been holding up well but he could feel himself losing it as he reached for the door handle.

'Odd Job?'

'What is it?' Vince turned around.

'Promise me something?'

'Anything.'

'Stay cheeky.'

'I will, Norman, I will.' Vince couldn't look at the Halfords as he made his way to the front door. He wanted to say something but the words were not there. He drifted in and out of sleep that night. It was just as he was getting dressed for work the next morning that he heard the phone ring and his mother answer. She came into his bedroom with tears in her eyes. She didn't have to say anything. She went over to her son and put her arms around him and he cried unashamedly on her shoulder.

Vince did not go to work that day. Instead he was to be found wandering over Brodie's fields and through the woods they had all played in when they were younger. He walked for miles lost in his thoughts, aimlessly going nowhere. He arrived back in the village late in the afternoon.

*

The funeral was three days later. The church was packed to capacity with as many mourners standing outside as there were seated inside. The service delivered by the Reverend Calder was one of his finest. Only his experience and his sense of duty prevented him from faltering on this sombre day. His rendition was magnificent from start to finish with the congregation hanging on to his every word. Norman's coffin was carried from the church to the graveside by the chums with whom he'd grown up. The lowering of his remains was reserved for his immediate family with the two remaining cords taken by Vince and Spike. Victoria left to prepare the pub with George and Betty following soon after. It would be one of their busiest days. Norman's mates were standing around trying their best to comfort one another.

'Are we going to the pub?' Wendy asked.

'Personally, I don't feel like going,' replied Podger. The others nodded.

'Odd Job, what do you say?'

'I don't want to go either. The thought of going for a drink is furthest from my mind. But we're going to have to go. If Norman's looking down, he's going to be well pissed off if we chicken out.'

'Odd Job's right. Come on, we're the Berrydale gang. Let's stop feeling sorry for ourselves. Let's just be glad that we were privileged to know the cheeky bugger.' That started the tears flowing again. Vince went over to Lucy and Alex who were comforting one another.

'When's this baby due then, Lucy?'

'Very soon. We're hoping for a boy.'

'Podge said you're getting a dog as well.'

'Well, when the baby comes along, I'm not going to be able to work for a while, so we've decided to get a puppy.'

'Will it be a farting dog?'

They all laughed.

*

'You OK, Vinz?'

'Yeah.'

'Yez very quiet thez days.'

'I'm OK.'

They had been busy with council business as usual. Vince was glad when four o'clock came around. He had his own car parked at the council building. The journey home would take ten minutes longer today. He had to make a detour past the off-licence. Spike also made a detour. His choice was the fishmonger's.

'Are you not having something to eat, Vincent?'

'No, Mum, I'm not hungry.'

'You weren't hungry last night either.'

'I had a sandwich earlier on. I'm fine really.'

'Are you going to the pub again tonight?'

'I thought I would walk down and see who's there.'

Spike and Harry were propping up the bar along with a few locals. The dart board was lit up and a game was in progress. Victoria was serving steak and kidney pie to a couple who were seated in the corner.

'Hi, Odd Job, how's it going?'

'OK, Victoria, how's it with you?'

'Just fine.'

'Are you having your usual, Vince?' George asked.

'Yeah, and give us a whisky as well, and a drink for these two,' he replied, pointing to the near empty glasses of Spike and Harry.

'What's new, Odd Job, still working for the council?'

'Yeah, yeah, still there. What have you two been up to?'

'Oh, you know. I'm keeping the Co-op on the straight and narrow. I'm spending more time in the shop now, doing a bit of selling. Speaking of selling, I'm putting the Capri on the market. I'm looking for a change.'

'Uh huh, that's good. Another whisky please, George.'

'Must be my round, I'll get these,' offered Harry. 'You wanting a pint as well, Odd Job?'

'Sure, why not.'

'How's Double Sandy?'

'Fine, I guess.'

'We haven't seen her around. You're still seeing each other, aren't you?'

'Yeah, yeah.'

'I was speaking to Mrs Halford yesterday. Have you seen her recently, Odd Job?' asked Harry.

'She and Norman's Dad were over visiting at the weekend. I saw them then.'

'I'll have to go and say hello. It's difficult knowing what to talk about.'

'Christ! Spike, since when have you been stuck for words?'

'Well...you know.'

'Yeah, it's difficult. Same again please, George.'

'Steady on, Odd Job. We've got to get up in the morning.'

'Yeah...so?'

'I'm fine with this pint, you and Spike go ahead.'

'Naw, I'm OK as well,' said Spike.

'Please yourselves. I'll have a whisky, George.'

It was closing time when Vince left the pub. Spike and Harry had gone home an hour earlier. Vince was at his bedroom door when Pamela called out, 'Alex phoned you, Vincent. Weren't you meant to meet her?'

'Yeah, Mum. I'll sort it out. Goodnight.'

'Goodnight, son.'

He found the glass where he had left it the previous night. He opened the drawer in the bedside cabinet and reached for the bottle.

'Hello, friend.'

'Hello, Vincent.'

The dream was the same as it had been the night before. They were on some distant island building a boat. Somehow Norman had been cast adrift and Vince could not reach the rope to pull him back to shore. He tried to run to the water's edge but his legs were heavy. He tried running backwards but could not make progress in this surreal landscape.

'Vincent, Vincent! Wake up. You'll be late for work.' Pamela was banging on his bedroom door. 'Are you going with your father?'

Vince jumped up in bed, the sweat running over his parched lips.

'What is it?'

'Your father's ready.'

'I'll take my own car today. Tell Dad I'll be there soon.' He was already reaching for his clothes, cursing the dryness in his mouth and the thumping headache. He quickly washed his face and under his arms and gulped down some cold water from the tap. The toothpaste helped to get rid of the taste of whisky.

'Are you having breakfast?'

'No time, Mum.'

'Here's your flask and sandwiches. You look terrible. You had a drinking session at the pub last night, didn't you?'

'Yeah, sorry, Mum. You know what the lads are like. Have we any aspirins?'

Vince arrived at the council building with no knowledge of how he got there. Charlie and Wilf had the engine of the van running,

'Youz been on the pizz again. Yez looks like shitz.'

'Yeah, yeah, let's get going before my father appears.'

They worked through the morning and Vince was glad when they stopped for the lunch-break. The aspirins hadn't helped to get rid of the fellow with the sledge hammer in his head.

'Drop me off at the bowling alley, Charlie. I'll walk or take the bus back. Cover for me if I'm late, will you?'

Alex was not amused at this sorry sight before her eyes. 'I phoned you last night. I thought we were going out, Odd Job. Look at you. You look like shite.'

'I'm sorry, Alex. I got caught up in a drinking session. I'll make it up to you.'

'You keep letting me down, Odd Job. I know your mates are important but I need to see you as well, or are you getting fed up of me?'

'Alex, please don't give me a hard time. I'm really sorry.'

'Well, I'm fed up with this...' She turned away.

'Can we go for a drive tonight?'

'I don't know. Look at the state of you. You can hardly walk.'

'I'm having a bad day...please!'

'I'm not sure.'

'Please!'

'OK, you can pick me up at seven?'

'Yes, of course,' he replied, sighing with relief. 'Seven it is. Have you any aspirins?'

'Here, take these.' She reached behind the counter for the packet.

He caught the bus back rather than walk. The day dragged past slowly for Vince. He managed to eat a sandwich and finish all of the tea in his flask. It was a relief when he finally parked his car at his house. He was too tired to look under the bonnet to investigate what the smell was that had started on the drive home. 'It'll be something electrical no doubt,' he thought, allowing himself a small curse as he headed for the front door. 'Bugger, what next?' He managed to eat some of the shepherd's pie that Pamela had put before him. Vince was relieved that Matthew was working late on some paperwork that had to be finished. He hadn't fancied a teatime conversation with his father.

'Is that all that you're having to eat?'

'I've ate most of it, Mum. I'm going to lie down for ten minutes.'

'OK, son.'

He was lost in his dream when he awoke with a start. He looked at his watch and could just see the dial in the darkness of his room. 'Damn!' he uttered as he leapt downstairs three at a time. Pamela was in the kitchen looking at a recipe in a magazine when she heard the commotion.

'Vincent, is that you?'

'It's me, Mum. Is it really ten o'clock? I've been sleeping.'

'Yes, I just left you. I thought that you had gone to bed. What is it?'

'I should have picked up Alex.' He reached for the phone in the hallway. There was no reply. 'Damn everything!' he said again as he went back to his room, cursing his stupidity. 'Why did I have to fall asleep? Damn!'

'Hello, friend.'
'Hello, Vincent.'

*

The pub was quiet that evening. Vince was on a mission to find Spike and fall out with him. It had taken three days to discover where the smell was coming from. Vince's first thoughts had been that it must be something electrical. A quick check did not show up anything obvious. The smell was getting worse and had it not been for Wilf's determination to get to the bottom of the problem they would have been stumped. Wilf and Charlie were having a good look under the bonnet at lunchtime when Wilf announced, 'Hez yez problem, Vinz. Yez can just sez it.' Wilf was pointing to the decomposing kipper that had once proudly swum in the Atlantic Ocean.

'Where?'

'Look, itz under there. Yez can just sez it.'

Vince leaned closer, holding his nose. He could just make out the tail fin sticking out from behind the intake tubes that sucked in the air for the heater. 'Spike! The shite! I know it was him. I'll kill him!' Vince found a rag and started to poke at the kipper which was lodged well in place. It didn't want to come out in one piece which, presumably, had been Spike's objective in the first place. It would be many days before the smell would go away.

Harry was at the bar. It had been a long day. He was on his second drink.

'Pint, Odd Job?'

'Yeah, where is the shite?'

'Who?'

'Spike, is he in the toilet?'

'Naw, he hasn't been in yet. What's wrong?'

'There's the small matter of a dead fish in my car. Did you know about it?'

'C'mom, Odd Job. How would I know about it?' he chuckled.

'Yeah, sure. You haven't seen Double Sandy going around have you?'

'Eh...no.'

'What is it? I know when you're lying.'

'Nothing.'

'Come on, Harry. What is it?'

'What's what, Odd Job?' asked Spike who'd arrived at the bar.

'I asked about Double Sandy and Harry's gone all funny on me and by the way, thanks for the fish. My car's still bloody honking.'

'Harry's probably dodging the question about Double Sandy.'

'What about her?'

Harry was looking the other way. He knew that diplomacy was not one of Spike's strong points.

'Well, what about her? Have you seen her?' Vince asked again.

'Yeah, I've seen her. She's been going out with someone.'

'Who?'

'Grommet.'

'Grommet! Is that right, Harry?'

'Yeah...well...I saw her in his car last night. She might've just been getting a lift, Odd Job...you know.'

'Yeah, yeah, sure, get's a whisky, George. Are you

certain it was her?'

'Positive. Have you two fallen out?'

'I was supposed to meet her and I fucked up. You know what women are like.'

'Have you tried phoning her?'

'Yeah, yeah, I've tried,' replied Vince, downing his drink in one gulp.

*

'You miss having him around, don't you, Vincent?'

'Yes, Mum, I do. He would have been twenty six this month.'

'I know. It's a shame...someone *so* young.'

'I miss Gran too, and her stout.'

'We all do. It's been a few years now. My, how time flies past. Your Grandad's been dead for such a long time. You won't remember too much about him, will you?'

'No, not a lot. He was well liked, wasn't he?'

'Yes, after he came home from the war he seemed to settle into the community very well. He got on with everyone. I remember when I was growing up he always liked to play games. He would hoist me up on his shoulders and pretend to be a horse. We would gallop off down the garden.' Pamela paused as she recalled her youth.

'Go on, Mum, tell me more.'

'There's not a lot to tell really. Times were hard in those days, a lot harder than you have had to experience. We didn't have the things that you have, although your Grandad always managed to get hold of sweets. He would hide them from me in the oddest of places, usually wrapped in a piece of newspaper. He would draw a shamrock to make it easier for me to find them. Sometimes he would put them down the sofa and leave a newspaper beside the seat with the drawing on it. Another favourite place was in the pile of kindling beside the fireplace. He would make his mark on the wood with a pencil. I was always looking in odd places in case there was a sweet to be found. He liked going on walks as well. He was always off somewhere with your Grandma and me. I would be up on his shoulders. I remember that I could see for miles from up there, or so it seemed,' she said with a sigh.

'Back then, were times really that hard?'

'Yes, they were. I can remember having to use hot water to make custard instead of milk. It wasn't until your Grandad started in the farming community that we had a supply of milk to drink and to make butter.'

'I don't suppose many do that now, do they?'

'No, I shouldn't think so. We have these supermarkets now. Times have changed. What are you up to tonight...meeting anyone?'

'I thought I'd walk down for a pint and see what's happening.'

'Have you been drinking a lot?'

'No more than anyone else. Why?'

'Oh, it's just that when I clean your room you always seem to have a bottle at hand.'

'Are you checking up on me?'

'I am your mother. Mothers worry, you know.'

'Stop worrying. I sometimes have a swig before bed. It helps me sleep, OK?'

'Are you and Alex serious about each other? You

never talk about her. There's no chance of a wedding, then?'

'We get on fine, Mum. We like things as they are. Why? Are you wanting rid of me? I'd try and get a flat in town but what's the point, I'm only half an hour away from work.'

'You don't want to have babies, then?'

'Naw, they're horrible smelly things. No, seriously, Mum, I like things as they are. Have you finished interrogating me now? I'm off for that pint.'

'Don't get involved in a drinking session. It's only Thursday. You've got work tomorrow.'

'I won't.'

Harry and Spike were settled in their usual spot, propping up the bar.

'Are you having a pint, Odd Job?'

'Yeah, I suppose so.'

'Fancy a game of darts?'

'Are you and Veronica still an item, Harry?'

'Yeah, why?'

'I'm just curious. Mum was asking me about my love life. I wondered if I was missing something.'

'Harry was saying earlier that he was looking for a flat in town,' said Spike.

'Oops, man overboard.'

'Let's have a game. Victoria, can you give us a wet cloth for this board?'

'Can't you use your tongue, Spike? It's usually hanging out of your mouth.'

'Victoria, honey bunch, you don't know what you're missing. You know I like my woman the same way as I like my tea.'

'I've never seen an ugly cup of tea.'

'I mean hot and sweet!'

'Are we playing this game of darts, or what?'

'Odd Job, you're getting to be a real grumpy shite. Here, have one of these to sweeten you up. Will I take the paper off for you?' said Spike, offering the bag of boilings.

'Odd Job! Vince! Hello, is anyone home?' Vince was standing rigid, staring at the wall. 'What was that Mum was talking about?' he thought.

'Odd Job, what's the matter? You look as if you've seen a ghost. Are you alright?'

'What!'

'Are you OK? I know I'm brilliant at darts but there's no need to be shitting yourself because you're about to play me. You and Harry have the first game. I'll mark the board. Odd Job! Are you listening?'

'Eh...I'm going to the bog...I'll be right back.'

'Harry, what's wrong with him?'

'I dunno.'

Vince was in the gents, leaning against the wall and gathering his thoughts. 'What was Mum saying about sweets and Grandad?'

'Odd Job, are you in there? Come on, you haven't got a woman in there, have you? Are you in the ladies by mistake...Odd Job!' Harry shouted.

'Yeah, yeah, I'm here. You play Spike and I'll play the winner.'

Vince was still in a dream as he stood beside the dartboard, holding the chalk.

'Well, come on Odd Job, that's two-sixty left.'
'What?'
'Forty-one from three o one leaves two-sixty. Christ! What's wrong with you tonight? Is Double Sandy giving you rations?'
'Sorry. I was miles away.'
'Give us the chalk. We'll mark the board ourselves. What's the matter with you?'
'Nothing, I was just thinking. I have to go home. I've just remembered something.'
'What is it? Have you forgotten to put your electric blanket on?'
'Yeah, yeah, yeah...I'll see you later.'
'What's up, Vince. Is the beer that bad?'
'I'll see you, George. Got to go.' He walked the short distance home. His mind was working overtime.
'You're back early. Was there nobody in the pub?'
'Spike and Harry are there. I left them playing darts. I thought I might have an early night. I'm just going to have a cuppa. You want one, Mum?'
'Yes, alright.'
Vince came back with two cups of tea. 'What's Dad doing?'
'He's pottering about in the shed. God knows what he's up to.'
'I was thinking about what you were saying earlier.'
'About what?' Pamela replied.
'About when you were a little girl and the games you played. It seems strange talking about it. I can't imagine you as a child. What did Grandad do with the sweets? Did you say he left a mark?'

'Yes, he would make one of his drawings to help me find them. It wasn't that difficult really.'

'It was a shamrock, you said?'

'Yes, it was always a shamrock. Why are you so interested, Vincent?'

'I just like hearing the stories about Gran and Grandad.'

'Your Gran, she could tell a good story. You used to like her stories, although she did exaggerate a bit now and again.'

'Yeah, they were good stories. I think I'll go and see what Dad's doing and then go to my bed. I've to tell him I'm taking my own car tomorrow. I've something to do at lunchtime.'

Vince found Matthew in the shed with a rag in his hand.

'What are you doing back, son. Has George closed the pub early?'

'Naw, I'm wanting an early night. What are you doing?'

'I'm oiling this mower.'

'I see you've got some of the council's oil there.'

'They won't miss it, perks of the job.'

'Dad, I'm taking my own car tomorrow. I won't need a lift. I've something to do at lunchtime.'

'Are you meeting that crazy girlfriend of yours?'

'Maybe, I'm off for an early night. I'll see you tomorrow.'

'Where are you working anyway? Have you finished down beside the academy?'

'Wilf thinks we'll be done by lunchtime and get the

rest of the day to tidy up the tools.'

'OK, I'll see you tomorrow. Sleep well, son.'

'Night, Dad.' Vince went back inside and put the cup in the sink.

'Night, Mum'

'Goodnight, Vincent.'

He reached for the phone in the hallway and dialled the number. Her Mum answered.

'Hello, it's Vince. Is Alex there?'

'No, Vince, she's out somewhere. I don't know where. I'll tell her you called.'

'OK, thanks.' He climbed the stairs and entered his room.

'Hello, Vincent.'

'Hello, friend.'

Friday morning was taken up with replacing of kerb stones at the academy where the bus stopped. Some drivers would park on the pavement to unload the school kids and over a period of time the paving slabs had become cracked and broken. Vince along with Charlie and Wilf worked on for another hour replacing the slabs. They didn't stop for lunch. This would enable them to get the job finished and get back to the depot earlier. That morning Vince had gone straight to where they were working and had his car parked round the corner.

'Whez you going? Off to sez your bird?'

'I've something to do. I'll see you back at the depot. Cover for me if I'm a bit late, will you?'

'Yez, OK.'

Vince was back in Berrydale in less than thirty minutes. He parked the car round the rear of his house, hoping he wouldn't bump into his Mum. He opened the shed and reached for his old and trusty bike. The back tyre was flat. 'Damn! I should have checked it last night,' he thought. 'This is going to waste time.' Fortunately the pump was at hand and the tyre only needed some air.

Vince was outside Ferguson's building in five minutes, having first checked that the farmer and his Land Rover were gone. He went over to the shed that held all the junk and opened the door. The hinges were well-worn now and the door had to be lifted slightly to open it. The chests were still there along with the potato sacks, some of which were still full. Vince went towards the wall where he had scratched the letter W that looked like Julie's boobs and stared at the shamrock that was still clear and visible. A strange, excited feeling was surging through his body as he ran his shaking fingers around the stone that held the drawing. The mortar was loose and did not require a lot of effort to dislodge. The stone moved as he held it with both hands, sticking his fingers as far into the cracks as he could. He pulled the stone and it came out more easily than he had expected, revealing a dark hole. He placed the stone carefully on the floor and peered into the darkness. He remembered how scared he'd been at some of the episodes of *Quatermass and the Pit* that he'd seen on television and imagined that some dark and evil force would grab his hand should he venture further inside. Vince peered into the darkness. He could see the outline of something that was just made visible by the aid of the meagre light that shone through the open door. His hands were still shaking as he reached in and clasped the box firmly to pull it out. It was quite a large container that had once been black but, with the passage of time, was now covered in rust. He laid the box down for closer examination. It had a lid that was hinged in two places with a key-hole that was minus the key. Vince pulled at the lid but it refused to budge. He glanced around but he could see nothing at hand that would enable him to get the box open. Vince realised that it was too large to carry on his bike and he would have to leave it for the moment. If he walked to his house there would be more chance of him being seen by someone. He decided that the best plan would be to come back with his car. He placed the box back into the dark hole and carefully replaced the stone, making sure that it was the correct way up. His Grandad had gone to a great deal of effort to enlarge the hole to make the box fit. He had removed the stone from behind as well. Vince packed some of the loose mortar back and kicked away the rubble that had fallen on the floor. As he reached for the door he turned around, looked at the wall and thought, 'Good old Grandma, I knew you were right.'

Vince closed the shed door behind him, squinting in the bright light. A glance at his watch told him he was late. He grabbed his bike and pedalled off with his heartbeat not quite back to normal. Vince almost collided with the dog that had appeared from nowhere. 'Christ! That's Brodie's dog,' he thought. 'What's it doing skulking around here?' He put his bike back in the shed and then went to his car for the journey back to town. His Mum was still nowhere to be seen. He thought that she must be visiting someone in the village.

'Whez you been? Yez late.'

'Sorry, lads. I got held up,' Vince replied, taking a

deep breath. His body was still not back to normal.

'Your Dad was round checking things out. We said you were in the toilet. Isn't that right, Wilf?'

'Yez.'

'Thanks, Charlie. What's to be done here? Are we tidied up for the weekend?'

'We've just to check these machines for fuel and oil and get the van filled up with diesel for Monday. Can you check the tyres on the back, Vince? I think the one on the left could do with some air. Vince! Are you listening? Have we got to do all the bloody work around here? You've already had an hour for lunch.'

'Hez been wiz hiz bird again.'

'What! The tyres, right, I'm doing it,' replied Vince. His thoughts were miles away.

Vince drove home that afternoon, thinking that he would have to wait another week before he could get back to Ferguson's place. He couldn't take the chance any other time. Friday was the only day that the farmer would be at the Mart. 'Damn!' he said out loud. It was going to be a long week.

*

Pamela was visiting Mrs Halford for their weekly cup of tea and a chat. On her way back she thought she noticed Vincent drive off, heading in the direction of town. Matthew had arranged for an electrician to call in past. They had decided to install a shower above the bath. Matthew did most of the handy work himself but the fuse box had to be upgraded to handle the extra load. He mentioned this to Grommet, one of the council's electricians. Grommet said he would call round that

Friday to install a new consumer unit. He would make it his last call and would take his own car rather than a council vehicle. Pamela had just finished making herself a cup of tea when he arrived in his red MGB GT. Grommet was a handsome, single man who was very popular with the ladies. He had a look that could melt a woman's heart. He just had to glance at them with his piercing, blue eyes and they were captivated. He had perfectly groomed hair and brilliant white teeth that went with his smile. Pamela answered the door to be confronted with this god.

'Mrs Wright?'

'Yes.'

'I'm Grommet, the electrician. Matthew asked me to call in past. Is it convenient?'

'Yes, of course,' she replied, fiddling with her hair. 'Come in, the bathroom's through there,' she pointed. 'Would you like a cup of tea?'

'That would be fine, thanks. Just milk, no sugar please.'

Pamela went to put the kettle on but first made a detour to the dressing table in her room to brush her hair. She came back with the tea and a plate of biscuits.

'Did I interrupt you?'

'What do you mean?'

'Your hair, you've brushed it. Did I interrupt you when I called? You washed it just in time. I'm going to switch the electric off.'

'I must look a mess. I haven't had time to tidy myself up today,' she said, adjusting the front of her dress. 'Um, is the tea OK?'

'Yes, it's lovely.'

'I'll let you get on. I'm holding you up. Why do they call you Grommet? What's your proper name?'

'It's Steve, actually. You know how these nicknames stick.'

'Oh,' she purred. 'Should I go and change my dress?' she thought. 'Pamela, stop acting like a school girl.'

He installed the new consumer unit and connected the wiring. Matthew had already run the wires to the shower unit, making the job relatively simple.

'How are you getting on? Would you like another cup of tea?'

'No thanks, I'm about finished. I've just got to do a mega test and I'll be on my way.'

'Do you have to go?' dreamed Pamela.

'Mrs Wright, come and have a look at how the shower works. You switch it on here, the one with the red light. That tells you the power is going to the shower and that's all there is to it.'

'Can we try it now, you handsome god? We could leave it on cold,' she wanted to cry. 'Well, that seems simple enough. We'll all be having showers now.'

'If you have any problems, get Matthew to give me a shout, OK?'

'What do I owe you, Steve?'

'Nothing, it's been taken care of. I'd better be going. It's been nice meeting you.' He rode off into the fading sunset in his red machine, leaving Pamela still fiddling with her hair. Matthew was home a couple of hours later.

'Has Grommet been?' he shouted as he came through the door.

'Yes, it's fixed. He didn't take long.'

'Good, we'll get a shower now. What have you done to your hair?'

'Nothing, why?'

'Oh, it looks different somehow.'

*

Friday couldn't come quickly enough for Vince. He was out with Wilf and Charlie, clearing a tree that had been blown over by the wind the night before. It was still blowing a storm as they attacked the old beech with the chainsaw. The sawdust from the cutting was swirling in the breeze, getting into their mouths and eyes. They only had one pair of goggles between them which were claimed by Charlie, leaving the other two uncomfortable with the debris that was flying around. Charlie was in charge of the chainsaw. Wilf and Vince were assisting but squinting with one eye open in case Charlie mistook one of their limbs for a branch.

The job was finished by eleven o'clock, with the tree sawn up and loaded in the back of the pick-up truck. They had to make two trips to collect all the logs and debris. Matthew instructed them to take one load to Wilf's house, the other load was dropped off at Charlie's place. It would make good firewood to burn along with the coal. The day had been easy for a change and they managed to get finished before lunchtime. Vince had taken his car to work. He decided that he would drive to Ferguson's during the lunch-hour, quickly load the box and be gone in a few minutes. If anyone spotted him and asked what his car was doing there, he would think up some excuse about one of Ferguson's cattle being out of the field. He slowed down beside the big tree he used to climb, to make sure there was no activity on the farm. There was nobody to be seen, which was to be expected on Mart day. Vince reversed his car to the shed door and quickly opened the boot. He pushed open the door and made straight for the stone wall, banging his knee on one of the chests. 'Ferguson's shifted this stuff around,' he thought, cursing his haste. He limped to the wall and grabbed the stone. He pulled it out and laid it at his feet. Vince reached inside for the box but could feel nothing there. He peered into the dark hole but could see no sign of the box he had inspected the week before. 'What the...' He felt again, right to the back and all around the sides. 'What's going on?' he thought, staring in disbelief at the dark hole. He sat down on one of the chests to gather his thoughts. He looked around in the gloom of the shed in the faint hope that something would offer a clue as to what was happening. Vince could feel the rage building inside him. He clenched his fists and banged them on the chest. Realising that nothing was to be gained by sitting there, he checked the cavity once more, before putting the stone back in place.

*

'Alex I need to talk to you.'

'I've told you, I'm busy.'

'Please! I need to see you badly.' This was Vince's umpteenth phone call to the bowling alley. He had been thwarted in his previous attempts, both by Alex and the other staff.

'Why won't you speak to me?'

'What's to speak about?'

'I miss you, I need to...' The line went dead.

Ferguson and Brodie were friendly enough neighbours. They would borrow the odd farm implement from one another as needs arose. Brodie was returning Ferguson's heavy hammer on the Friday, having borrowed it to repair a part of the fencing that held in his sheep. He left the tractor and cart in the field and walked the short distance to return the hammer to Ferguson's shed. It was when he rounded the corner of the building that he noticed the person on the bike going down the farm road. He made a mental note to mention it to Ferguson when he came back from the Mart.

Vince parked his car in the bowling alley car park. He took a deep breath and walked through the main door. It was five minutes before the time that Alex would normally break for lunch. Alex looked up at Vince from behind the kiosk.

'Alex, I need to talk to you.' He thought he saw a smile on her face. His voice wavered as he was reminded of how beautiful she was.

'What are you doing here, Odd Job?'

'Can I talk to you? Are you going on your lunch break?'

'Yes, but I was going shopping.'

'It won't take long. My car's in the car park.'

'OK, five minutes. That's all.'

'Thanks.' Vince reached over for the flowers that were in the back seat and handed them to Alex. 'These are for you...I didn't know what to get you.'

'You got me flowers? I've never had flowers before. They're...they're lovely. Thank you.'

'Alex, I know that I'm an arsehole and I haven't

treated you right. It's just...it's just that I've been a bit messed up lately, what with everything going on...Norman and...you know...'

'We all miss him. Not just you, Odd Job.'

'I know, I know, I'm sorry. Is it true about you and Grommet?'

'What?'

'You know...'

'We've been out a couple of times.'

'And?'

'Well, what do you expect me to do? Sit around waiting for you to maybe show up!'

Vince hung his head. 'Are you serious about him?'

'No...No! He's a ladies' man. He just happened to be around at the time.' She looked at Vince with tears in her eyes. She had never imagined that he could look as sad as he did at that moment. 'I hear you've been drinking a lot.'

'So...who cares? Did you and Grommet...you know?'

Alex looked down at the bunch of flowers in her lap. 'It was nothing. It didn't mean anything. He's a shite.'

'So am I.'

Alex smiled. 'Yeah, I know.'

'Can we see each other again, if you're free?'

'I don't know. I really...'

The sadness was back in his eyes. They both stared out of the window in silence.

'Alex, I need you around. I miss you.'

'How's Tonto? Is he asking for me?'

'Don't know. I can never understand what he's saying. I don't speak Indian.'

She laughed. She knew then what it was that she

wanted.

'Have you got time for me to tell you a story?'

'Depends, I can't afford the Legion fees.'

Vince told Alex about the gold coins and how he and Norman had set about trying to find them. He told her the whole story about how he had finally found the box at Ferguson's and described his frustration on returning to find that it had gone.

'Is this true, Odd Job? It's a bit far-fetched.'

'It's true. Can you help me find these bloody coins?'

'Is that what you want?'

'Yes.'

'What's that smell? Have you coughed in your pants?'

'It was Spike. He hid a dead fish under the bonnet. I can't get rid of the stench.'

'I suppose he's still a tart, is he?'

'Yeah, he's a bit of a rascal alright. What about the shopping you were supposed to be doing?'

'I'll do it another day.'

'Can I pick you up tonight?'

'Yes, as long as you put me down gently. You will show up, won't you?'

'I promise. What about Grommet?'

'Why? Do I have to ask him along as well?'

'You know what I mean.'

'I've told you...he's history. Have I hurt you?'

'It's my own fault, Alex.'

'Can I make it up to you?'

'I'll think of something.' He grinned. 'We'd better get back to work. I'll see you tonight, then?'

'Yes.' She leaned over and gave him a kiss on the

cheek.

*

Vince could hardly wait to see Alex. It seemed that the day dragged on slower than ever. He picked her up at her house and they parked on a piece of waste ground near the edge of the town to discuss their plans for the evening. Vince couldn't keep his hands off Alex. She looked ravishing.

'We could go for a drive and gaze at the stars.'

'Oh yeah. You've painted stars on the inside of the car roof, have you?'

'We don't have to stay in the car. We could lie on the grass.'

'In which case, you wouldn't get to see the stars, Odd Job, but I bet *I* would.'

'You could describe them to me as I look into your beautiful eyes.'

'What are you doing?'

'I'm trying to find the combination to your knickers. Are they glued on?' he replied.

'My prince, you only have to look at me and they will fall off. Stop doing that. We're supposed to be discussing where we're going. How can we speak when you're trying to ravish me?'

'I cannot help it, my beautiful pumpkin. You have taken me to places I've never been before.'

'OK, so we went to the zoo, so what?'

'I meant heaven, you wild and passionate creature.'

'Heaven would be nice but let's get tonight over with first. Stop playing with my breasts.'

'I was just doing a stock check.'

'And?'

'They all seem to be there but a closer inspection would be appreciated. Are you not in the mood for romance?'

'Odd Job! Will you stop that?' Her blouse was off by now.

'Nobody will see us. It's getting dark.' He started on her other garments. She was pretending not to enjoy it.

'We could go for a meal and have a *giraffe* of wine.'

'Whatever you say, my pumpkin,' Vince murmured. 'A *giraffe* of wine would be nice.'

'I'm going to end up naked again, aren't I?'

'I was counting on it.' She was down to her pants by now.

'My, what a wonderful magician you are, Odd Job,' she thought.

'We could go bowling.'

'Bowling! I work in that place all week and you want to take me there on my night off. I'm a sensitive woman. I need to be spoiled. Whisk me away to paradise now. Book me into a hotel by the River Seine in Paris. I could leave my clothes off just to save time. How fast do the council mowers go? We could be in Paris by ten... Let's just go for a drink.'

'Where do you want to go, The Prince Albert?' asked Vince, nuzzling her neck.

'All your chums will be there as usual. Fat chance I'll have of getting you on your...your own...ooh that's nice...you're such...ooh...we could...ooh later.

*

The next day, somewhere in town, Lucy gave birth to a

healthy eight pound three ounce baby. He was to be named Norman Vincent Chalmers.

*

'So what do you think?'

'About what?'

'The gold coins, of course.' Vince had gone to the bowling alley to speak to Alex at lunch time. They were seated in Vince's car in the car park. He was determined to get to the bottom of this mystery.

'You said that you saw Brodie's dog that day?'

'Yes, I'm sure it was his dog. Do you think Brodie has the box?'

'Well, go and ask him.' Alex was kissing a particularly sensitive area on Vince's neck.

'Alex!'

'What?'

'Can you stop that? You said you were going to help me find these dammed coins. I'm trying to concentrate.'

'I'm helping you to relax, my prince. Have you asked Tonto. He might have an idea?'

'This is serious for God's sake. I have to find that box.'

'Alright, why don't we just go and ask him and share the booty?'

'That's silly.'

'Oh well, I'm only a girlie. I can't help it if I'm not a qualified treasure hunter,' she said, pulling one of her faces. 'Can I go back to munching on your neck? I've still to do the other side.'

'We'll have to go and see Brodie and somehow find out if he knows anything.'

'Do you want me to distract him?'

'What do you mean?'

'I could flash my knickers while you go and search his house.'

'Alex, are you ever serious?'

'Listen, it's pretty serious if I show my underwear in public. I wouldn't do it normally.'

They finally agreed that they would go to Brodie's that weekend to see if they could find out anything more about the box.

*

The weekend came and the walk to Brodie's took them twenty minutes. They stopped several times and kissed and reminisced about the day they'd joined *The Stupid Grin Club*.

'I was the first wasn't I?' asked Vince.

'Yes, you were...that day anyway.'

'Alex!'

'Of course you were, stupid.'

'Now you tell me I was stupid.'

'That as well.'

Brodie was tinkering with his tractor as they approached. Vince reflected on how old he looked compared to the sprightly man they had known all those years ago. His back was now hunched, a legacy of years of hard work. His hair was grey and thinning.

'Hello, you two. What are you up to, then?'

'Oh, just out for a walk. How are you keeping?'

'Just trying to keep this bloody machine working. I should get a new one but I can't afford it.'

'It's done a lot of work, hasn't it?'

'Yes, it'll see me out.'

'You're not thinking about retiring?' asked Alex.

'Me, retire! No bloody chance.'

'You haven't got a secret hoard of cash, have you?'

'I wish. Ferguson's the one who'll be retiring, not me.'

'Oh, why's that?'

'Well, I shouldn't be speaking about this but he seems to have come into some money.'

'Money?'

'Well, not exactly money. He was on about something he'd found that was going to make him rich. He didn't say what. Probably some piece of old furniture lying around that he thinks is an antique. You know how much junk he has lying around. He told me not to mention it to anyone, so don't say anything, will you?'

'No, we won't say a word,' said Alex.

'Well,' said Vince. 'We won't hold you up. We'd better be getting along. We'll see you soon.'

'Enjoy your walk. Bye for now,' said Brodie.

Alex and Vince turned and headed back down the field that ran beside the wood.

'Well, well, what do you think of that?'

'I was disappointed.'

'What do you mean, Alex?'

'Well, you know. I didn't get to show my knickers. Does this mean that I'll have to flash them to Ferguson?'

'It can only mean that he must have found the box.'

'Shall we go through the wood?'

'What for?'

'You know, I really had my heart set on showing my panties to someone. I've had a good look round and you seem to be the only one available, Odd Job.'

Vince grinned as he took her hand and led her off to the wood.

*

Ferguson returned from the Mart that day, and Brodie had mentioned that he'd noticed someone on a bicycle but didn't see who it might have been. After some talk about the price of cattle and when Brodie had gone, Ferguson entered the shed that held the potato sacks. The light from the doorway shone on the wall and he noticed that something looked odd. On closer inspection he saw that the stone with the drawing on it looked different. He stepped up to the wall and heard the crunch of masonry under his feet. He wondered why the dry mixture had fallen away and the rest of the wall was undisturbed. He felt around the stone and was surprised to find it loose. It came away and crashed to the floor just missing his boots. He looked into the dark hole and noticed the outline of a box. He found a hammer and chisel which made short work of the rusty lock and gazed in disbelief at the contents.

*

'We'll just have to go to Ferguson's and have a rummage around to see what we can find out,' said Alex as she sat with Vince in the car.

'And how do you suggest that we do that? He's not likely to have the box in a shed with a sign on it saying *Treasure,* is he?' replied Vince, raising his voice.

'Don't get mad at me. I'll do my girlie thing and cry if you want.'

'I'm sorry, Alex, it's just that I'm fed up with this

bloody gold coins thing. It seems to have been going on forever. We don't even know what's in the box, for Christ's sake!'

'Maybe it's just your Grandad's sandwiches.'

'Alex!'

'Sorry.'

'I'm going to have a look on Friday. I'll sneak away at lunchtime. What about you?'

'I'll phone in sick if you want and take the whole day off.'

'What will you say is wrong with you?'

'I'll think of something. We girlies have lots of things to put up with. I could tell them that my menstrual cycle has a puncture.'

'I could pick you up.'

'Yeah, will I need a disguise?'

'How quick can you grow a beard?'

'Christ! I'm shaving now. Whatever next?' said Alex as she leaned over to nibble on Vince's ear.

Vince had no problem sneaking away at lunchtime on Friday and was in the car heading back to Berrydale with Alex in the front beside him. Alex had phoned her supervisor to say that she had been up all night being sick. She was dressed in a trench coat that had been hanging in the wardrobe for quite a while. On her head was a beret that had once been worn by her mother. When Vince had picked her up his sombre expression had changed the moment she opened the door. She would not have looked out of place in a Peter Sellers film.

'You didn't fancy the beard, then?'

'I shaved it off at the last minute. It just wasn't me.'

The two of them parked the car and headed straight for the shed that held the chests and potato sacks. Vince pulled out the stone and pointed to the empty hole behind.

'Look! I told you. Here it is,' he said to Alex.

'I believe you, Odd Job, I believe you. I never doubted your story,' she replied.

'There was a black box in here and this is what we need to find,' said Vince, feeling slightly agitated. 'I'm going to look in the other shed. You have a good look in here. I'll be back soon.' Vince turned and went through the half-open door and headed for the other building.

Alex was sprawled on top of one of the chests and was looking inside the one behind it when she heard the footsteps.

'You're back quick, Odd Job. Did you get scared on your own?'

'What do you think you're doing?' asked the gruff voice from behind and to the left.

'Wha...who is that?' asked a startled Alex, realising the voice didn't belong to Vince. She spun round and faced the figure holding the double-barrelled shotgun.

'Mr Ferguson, it's you!' Vince and Alex had seen no sign of the farmer when they had arrived earlier. They knew that Friday was Mart day and they should have been undisturbed for most of the day.

'Who are you and what are you doing in my shed?'

'Eh..um...eh...it's Alex... Alexandria...Double Sandy.'

'You're Vincent Wright's friend, aren't you?'

'Eh...maybe...yes,' she replied, struggling for words.

'Well! What are you doing here, girl?'

'It's a long story,' was her squeaky reply. 'Odd Job,

where are you?' she whispered under her breath.

Vince had looked everywhere in the cow shed for the box. He was glad to get back outside into the fresh air away from the smell of the building. He was leaning on the wall beside the door when he saw Ferguson's Land Rover parked beside the house. He hadn't noticed it before so he presumed that the farmer had just arrived.

'Bugger! What next?' He turned swiftly to head in the direction of Alex and stopped in his tracks as he came upon the figure in the doorway. Vince could see from an angle that Ferguson was holding a shotgun. His second thought was to jump on the farmer. His first was more important.

'Alex! Are you OK?' he shouted.

'Ye...yes,' she replied.

Ferguson spun round at the sound of the voice. He was now pointing the gun at Vince.

'Well, well, so there are two of you, are there?'

'Hello, Mr Ferguson, nice weather for the time of year,' Vince replied along with a false smile.

'I was just asking this young woman what she was doing here,' Ferguson said, pointing the gun back in the direction of Alex.

'Don't point that gun at her!'

'What!'

'You heard. Point it at me if you want, or better still why don't you put it down. It's not as if we're strangers.'

'Alright then, tell me what you're up to,' he replied, un-cocking the hammerhead action of the old shotgun.

'We're looking for a box my Grandad hid in your shed. It belongs to me.'

'Oh does it now. Is that what you think?'

'Yes, have you seen it?'

'Maybe.'

'Well, have you got it or haven't you?' Vince was getting impatient. Maybe it was because he had now involved Alex in this unfolding drama.

'Yes I have. It's in the house, stashed in a safe place.'

'It belongs to my family,' continued Vince.

'It's on my property,' was the smug reply. 'Why don't I just shoot you both, eh?'

Vince was contemplating this statement. It seemed a little far-fetched that Ferguson would even think about such a deed.

'You can't just...' Vince stopped as he caught the expression on Alex's face. She was distracted by the cloud of dust that was forming in the distance as she looked over Vince's shoulder.

'Christ! I hope it's Skippy,' she murmured under her breath.

They all turned and saw the outline of Brodie's tractor bobbing up the dusty track, his dog running in front, announcing their arrival.

'Well, what about the box? Can I have it?' Vince asked with a renewed confidence.

'No, you can't. It belongs to me. It's on my property. We'll speak no more about it.'

Brodie came to a halt, the throttle of his tractor shut down. 'Hello, everybody. Have you been shooting rabbits?'

'Yes, I'm about to. These two youngsters were just leaving, weren't you?' Ferguson replied, staring at the two of them.

'Come on, Alex,' Vince said. They crept past the gun-toting farmer and were glad when they were out of the shed.

'Are you OK?' They were in the car and heading for the main road.

'I think so,' Alex replied. 'I was scared there for a while.'

'He wouldn't have shot us,' Vince laughed.

'Oh, that's reassuring. I shouldn't have messed my panties then.'

'We know the box is in the house. He said so.'

'Yeah, he did. He'll be on his guard now,' agreed Alex.

'What do you think?'

'We'd better resolve this soon. I don't have that many pairs of knickers left.'

'I'd better get back to work,' said Vince.

'Do you have to, my prince? I'm off sick you know. I have to be looked after. Won't you come back to my house and give me some care?'

Vince grinned as he took the turning that led to the other side of town.

Chapter Fifteen
A Treasure Hunt.

Vince managed to get back to his work. He had left Alex at her house. She was going to sneak out and do some shopping, hoping that no one would see her in her alleged sickly condition. The trench coat and beret with the dark glasses would help.

'Yez back, then, whez yez been this time? Yez never bloody hez.'

'Give us a break, Wilf. I've been busy.'

'Sure, yez been bizzy,'

'I was on a mission, OK?'

'OK, bizzy, bizzy, bizzy.'

'Let's get going.'

'Sure yez wouldn't like tez go home for a rest? Yez been hez for at lez five minutes now!'

'OK, stop taking the piss!'

They worked the afternoon with Wilf muttering, 'Bizzy, bizzy, bizzy,' anytime that Vince was within earshot. Charlie wasn't saying much but was chuckling away to himself in the background.

Vince was thinking hard about the day's events as he walked through the door for his supper. Pamela was at the cooker.

'Supper won't be long. We'll start without your Dad. He'll be along later. Did you hear about Ferguson?'

'What!' Vince had been half listening to his mother talking. The mention of Ferguson had his attention.

'What about him?'

'He's dead!'

'Dead!'

'Yes, dead. He shot himself!'

'What do you mean shot himself?'

'Well, they're not exactly sure what happened. They think it was an accident with the gun. It went off when he was going over the fence. Brodie found him. The police have been there all afternoon.'

'Christ!' Vince sat down on the chair, gathering his thoughts.

'We will get the full story soon, no doubt. Where are you going?' Vince had risen from the chair and was heading for the door.

'I'm going to see what I can find out.'

'What about your supper?'

'Can you put it in the oven for me? I won't be long.'

Vince wandered over to the end of Ferguson's road. There were still one or two people from the village standing talking, left over from the small crowd that had gathered earlier. A constable from town was stationed at the end of the road. There was only one police car left up at the farm. The ambulance had been and gone along with the forensic van. Vince approached the constable who was standing with his arms folded. He was obviously bored, having been standing at this point for some time with no relief from any of his colleagues.

'What happened to Ferguson?'

'I'm not allowed to say exactly,' the constable replied.

'Is Ferguson dead?'

'Yes, he is and that's all I'm allowed to tell you.'

'I was talking to him earlier at lunchtime.'

'What, today?'

'Yes.'

'You'd better have a word with the inspector. He's up there with Mr Brodie.'

Vince made his way up the road, trying to formulate in his mind what he was going to say. He saw no reason to mention the coins or to admit why he had been there earlier. He met the policeman and Brodie coming out of the shed.

'Who are you and what are you doing here? How did you get past the constable at the end of the road?'

Vince looked at this arrogant person with the uniform and fancy buttons. He could never tell the difference between the inspectors and superintendents. He knew the ones with the stripes were the sergeants. Vince was not very fond of any of them since the time he'd had a whack round the ear a few years before. He'd been cycling with Norman on the handlebars of the bike when a policeman had stopped them and administered the punishment.

'The policeman at the end of the road said to come up and speak to you. I told him that I was here at lunchtime speaking to Ferguson. What happened to him?'

'He shot himself with that gun of his, going over a fence. He's probably had the gun cocked ready to shoot rabbits. He always did that. You've seen his shotgun. The bloody thing is ancient,' blurted out Brodie, hardly drawing breath.

The inspector glared at the farmer. 'Mr Brodie was filling me in on the events of today. Where do you fit in, exactly?'

'I was here earlier and was just leaving when Mr Brodie arrived.'

'That's right. He and his girlfriend were leaving when I got here.'

Another glaring look was directed at Brodie. 'And what exactly were you and your girlfriend doing here?' asked the inspector.

'Nothing, really, we were just talking. Is there anything wrong with that?'

'No I don't suppose so,' was the quick reply before Brodie had a chance to talk. 'Mr Ferguson wasn't upset or anything when you saw him. Was he?'

'No, I don't think so.'

'OK, if we need to talk to you or your girlfriend, we'll come and get a statement. I have your name. Otherwise this looks like an unfortunate accident. I have to be back at the station. I'll bid you good day.' The inspector went down the dusty road in his shiny black car, leaving Vince and Brodie standing watching.

'So, it was you who found him?' Vince asked.

'He went to shoot rabbits just after you left. I went away soon after. It was about half-past two when I looked over to that field there and saw him slumped on the ground. I thought he'd had a heart attack or something. It wasn't until I got to him that I saw the blood. There was nothing I could do so I phoned the police. I don't know what will happen now. I've locked the house and put the key under a pot at the front door. He has no relatives as far as I know,' said Brodie, shaking his head.

'Uh huh.' Vince was thinking about keys and pots.

'Well, no good standing around here. Best get off home, I suppose. See you later, lad.'

'Yeah, see you later.' Vince's Dad was home when he arrived back at the house.

'What's the latest on Ferguson?' asked Matthew.

Vince told his Mum and his Dad about the events of the day while they were eating their supper. He was now eager to get to the phone.

'I'm just going to call Alex,' he said, rising from his chair. Her Mum answered the phone and after brief pleasantries, Vince was telling Alex what had happened.

'Can I pick you up?'

'When?'

'Tonight.'

'I was going to wash my hair.'

'Alex, never mind about your hair. Can I pick you up?'

'OK, give me an hour.'

'Have you got a torch you could bring?'

'You know I always carry one for you, my prince.'

'Alex!'

'Yes, I'll bring one. Now bugger off. I'll see you in an hour.'

After some serious thinking, Vince decided what it was he had to do. He would pick up Alex and go over the events of the day again in case he had missed anything out, then they would go to Ferguson's under cover of darkness. He was at her house by eight o'clock. She came through the door, wearing the trench coat and beret and holding a torch, her newly-washed hair following behind.

'What adventure are we to embark on tonight, my prince?' she asked, switching on the torch and holding it under her chin.

'You're scaring me,' joked Vince.

'Give me more time. I haven't started yet.'

'Are you willing to go with me to Ferguson's?'

'Christ! That was quick. Funerals aren't usually held that soon and I thought they were done in daylight.'

'Alex! Show some respect.'

'Sorry, just my attempt at humour, I'm not very good at it.'

Vince explained that they would go and look in Ferguson's house when it was dark. They would have to take the chance while they could. Alex was nodding her head in agreement, while trying to pull as many scary faces as she could with the aid of the torch. They parked the car in the lane usually reserved for lovers and after a lot of kissing and cuddling, it was dark enough for them to start walking the rest of the way. The night was calm with the occasional shaft of light as the moon danced behind the clouds. The silence was broken only by the distant call of an owl. They could see the faint glimmer from Brodie's window in the distance. They slowly made their way up the road in the direction of Ferguson's, scared to talk in case their voices would carry on the still, evening air. The monotonous hoot of the owl was the only sound to be heard above their heavy breathing. Vince could feel Alex tense from time to time as she followed behind. He gave her hand a reassuring squeeze to calm her nerves.

'I wish that bloody owl would sing a new song. It's making me nervous.'

'Shh, Alex!'

The outline of the farm building finally loomed in front of them. They stopped to catch their breath.

'Odd Job?'

'Shh!'

'Odd Job,' she whispered. 'You're hurting my hand. Stop squeezing so hard!'

'Sorry,' he whispered back.

'You should have brought Tonto with you. He'd be able to see in the dark.'

'Shh!'

'Shh yourself! I should be at home, having babies, doing knitting.'

'Will you shut up or I'll have to gag you.'

'Mmm, bondage. I've read about that in books.'

'Now listen, Alex. The key should be under the pot at the front door. Let's try to find it.'

'Oh good, I'll get a pee at the same time. I'm nearly wetting myself.'

The key was under the second of the two pots they tried. Vince was only switching on the torch for a few seconds at a time. He was aware that any light, no matter how small, would be seen from a long way off. The key turned in the lock and the door opened with an eerie squeak.

'The curtains. Make sure the curtains are properly shut and we can use the torch,' Vince said to Alex.

'They're shut.' Alex checked to see that they met in

the middle. She now had her torch switched on. The room was surprisingly tidy with barely any furniture apart from a sofa and two matching chairs and a table that stood beside the coal fire. They opened the only cupboard to reveal some tins and a packet of cereal.

'There's nothing much here. Let's check upstairs but make sure the curtains are drawn in all the rooms,' Vince whispered to Alex.

'Don't leave me on my own.'

'I won't. We'll check everything together.'

The upstairs rooms were just as sparse as downstairs, lacking any of the comforts of home. They didn't take long to check the two rooms thoroughly before going back downstairs to look in the spare room, the kitchen and the toilet as well.

'What now?' asked Alex.

'I don't know. Give me time to think.' Vince sat down on the sofa. Alex moved over to join him, the floor creaking as she did so.

'What was that?'

'What?'

'That noise.'

'What noise?'

'That creaking noise. Go back again.'

'It's only a floorboard.'

Alex stood over the spot and moved her foot back and forth, making the sound return. 'This noise?'

'Yeah, that's a loose floorboard. Keep standing there, will you?' Vince moved the chair out of the way to give him more room. He rolled back the carpet where Alex's foot was.

'Move your leg.' The carpet was rolled back further to reveal the floorboards. Vince handed the torch to Alex and then pulled up the loose board. The light from the torch lit up the black box beneath. He reached down and pulled it out. It was smaller than he remembered. Ferguson had removed the lock leaving some fresh scratches on the lid. Vince gingerly opened the hinged lid to reveal the contents.

'Yes! At last!'

Alex leaned over his shoulder, eager to see what all the fuss was about.

'Look! It's full of coins,' laughed Vince.

'No sandwiches then? Pity.'

'Let's get out of here, leave the place as we found it.' The carpet and sofa were returned to their original position. The curtains were checked, the door locked and the key returned to the flower pot. They were both glad to be out in the fresh air. They walked back the way they had come, moving faster this time, the occasional light from the moon guiding them. They were both shaking with excitement when they arrived at the car. Vince had another look in the box, before placing it in the boot of his car. Nothing was said until they were both seated inside.

'Christ! We've broken the law you know!'

'I've only taken what's rightfully mine, Alex.'

'Oh good, I like happy endings. Can we get away from here?' Alex locked her door. She imagined that a face would appear at the window, the longer they sat there in the darkness.

'Where will we...?'

'Just drive the bloody car!' she shouted.

Half an hour later they were parked in a side street in town. Alex had wanted to get away from Berrydale as quickly as possible.

'Do you think anyone saw us?'

'No, we're home and dry. Christ! I could murder a pint.'

'What now?'

'I'm going to get the box out of the boot and have a closer look.' Vince came back with some of the coins in his hand and set about examining them under the light that was coming from the street.

'They're in German,' said Alex.

'Of course they're in German. They're German gold coins, silly.'

'Oh, pardon me. What are they worth?'

'I don't know yet,' Vince murmured as he held one up to study.

'Are you happy now, Odd Job? Now that you've found your treasure.'

'Yeah, it's been a while, but worth the wait.' He held some of the coins up in the air just in case Grandma should be looking down at that moment. Vince and Alex said their goodnights and Vince set off on the drive home. It was late when he walked into the house. Matthew was still up.

'Hello, son. What have you been doing?'

'Nothing much. What's this junk doing here in the lobby?' asked Vince, almost tripping over the boxes that were stacked behind the door.

'It's your Mum. She's decided to tidy up the loft. She only started an hour ago then she went to bed. A lot of the stuff belonged to your Gran. The loft has badly needed cleaning out for ages. There are chests that have been up there for God knows how many years.'

'I'll lend a hand on Saturday, if you like.'

'I'm sure your Mum will appreciate the help. I'll tell her if she's still awake.'

Vince convinced his Mum to hold on until the weekend so that he could lend a hand. He planned to sneak into the loft with the gold coins and hide them in one of the chests that had still to be opened. They would be discovered sometime on Saturday, much to everyone's surprise. The next day Vince walked into the pub in the evening along with Spike, Harry and Podger.

'Four pints of Guinness please, George.'

'Guinness?'

'Yeah, that's right.'

'Why are we drinking Guinness, Odd Job?' asked Harry.

'It was good enough for my Grandma so it's good enough for us, OK?'

'Fine, OK, I'll give it a go.' The stout was poured and passed round.

'Cheers, Gran,' said Vince, raising his glass.

'Yeah, cheers,' said the others, with puzzled looks.

The night wore on with the four of them downing a few more pints of the stout before going home. The day after finishing tidying the loft with his Mum, Vince had arranged to meet Alex in town but first he made a small detour past the church-yard.

'We found them, Norman. We found them at last.' Vince was looking down at the headstone that bore the name of his chum. He lifted the withered flowers from the vase and cursed that he could not replace them with fresh ones. He gave the stone a wipe with his sleeve and vowed that next time he would bring fresh flowers. 'We all miss you, Norman, we all miss you terribly,' he whispered, turning away as the memories flooded back.

Chapter Sixteen
A Surprise for Spike.

Vince was at the scrap-yard, looking for a spring for his trailer. He was wandering around when he heard the words, 'Whatyewant?'

'I'm looking for a spring for the trailer. It was a caravan chassis originally. Have you got anything?'

'What size and how many leaves?' Patrick growled. He was eager to get back to the job he was doing.

'I've written the size on this,' said Vince, handing the piece of paper to the black blob that was Patrick's hand.

'Right, I'll have a look,' he grunted.

While Patrick was looking for the spring, Vince cast his eye over the cars that were stacked beside an old army truck: a burned out Granada; an Astra with the roof missing; and a nearly new Rover that had once been someone's pride and joy. He was wondering what sad stories lay behind the demise of these vehicles, when he found himself staring at a wrecked black Capri. The idea was formed in an instant.

'That Capri over there,' Vince shouted to Patrick. 'What happens to it now?'

'Goes in the crusher,' was the gruff reply.

'How much do you want for it?'

'It isn't for sale, goes in the crusher.'

'Well, what's it worth to you?'

'What do you want it for?' snarled Patrick.'

'Spares.'

'Spares! You don't have a Capri. You've a Cortina, haven't you? Me, I wouldn't have one myself. Too bloody thirsty on the petrol.'

'I want it for another reason,' Vince continued. 'I'll give you five quid for it.'

'Naw, I'll have to move them two cars off the top. It's not worth the bother.'

'Look, I'll move it myself if you let me use the fork-lift.'

'Twenty quid.'

'Seven!'

'Ten, and I'll throw in this,' Patrick said, holding a rusty spring that he had managed to find.

'Done,' smiled Vince.

Harry met up with Vince a little later in the day. 'Harry, can you do me a favour? I need your help with something.'

'What is it?'

'I need you to come with me to Patrick's yard.'

'Are you going into the scrap business? You've got a good start with that pile of rubbish you're driving.'

'There's a smashed Capri in Patrick's yard exactly like Spike's, same colour, same alloys. What night is he playing darts?'

A grin spread rapidly across Harry's face. He was digesting this very quickly. 'You shite! Are you having the plates made up as well?'

'Yup.'

'How exactly are you going to do it?'

'Watch and learn, my friend, watch and learn.' Harry's grin grew bigger as Vince went over the plan.

'Why can't Patrick help you load it?'

'He said he'd let me use his fork-lift. You know what a grumpy old moan he is.'

'OK,' said Harry who still had the grin. 'You shite!' he said again.

*

The darts team hadn't been doing very well and tonight they faced the lads from The Burnside Arms with their pretty, matching blue shirts.

'Tell me again,' said Harry.

'I'll ask about his Capri and get a drive in it. He is still selling it, isn't he?'

'As far as I know, but he'll want to go with you. Have you got the plates done?'

'They're in the boot of my car. We'll change them when we get the wreck loaded. Let's go, we only have a couple of hours.'

After the smashed car at Patrick's yard was loaded on to the trailer, they drove away and parked behind Vince's house. They then replaced the number plates front and back. Vince turned to Harry. 'You get down to the pub before they start the darts and find out when Spike is playing his singles. Come out the back and tell me five minutes before he's due on. I'll have this car ready and out of sight.'

'OK, Odd Job,' grinned Harry.

Vince was sitting behind the pub, looking at his watch and thinking, 'I hope Harry hasn't got involved in a drinking session. He should have been out by now.' As if on cue, Harry came running round the corner still wearing the grin.

'He's on next. You have about five minutes.'

'OK, when I get the keys off him, you pretend to go to the toilet and come and help me.'

'Hi, Spike, how's it going? Are you winning?' asked Vince as he walked in.

'I'm on next.'

'Have you sold that pile of shite yet?' Vince had made sure earlier that Spike's car was parked where expected.

'Fuck you!'

'I'll tell you what. Give me the keys. I might be able to shift it for you. I need to see how it drives.'

'If you hold on until I'm finished this game. I'm on next. Who's interested in it anyway?'

'Give me the bloody keys. I'm in a hurry. I won't be long. Do you want to be stuck with it for another month?'

'Spike, you're on!' the darters shouted.

'OK, here's the keys,' said Spike.

'Fine, I'll be right back,' said Vince, casting a glance at Harry who was heading for the door unnoticed. All the attention was on the next match.

'Right, jump in, we'll drive round the back and get the wreck,' said Vince as he started up Spike's car. They parked it out of sight and then jumped into Vince's car and trailer and drove it round to the front. They off-loaded the wrecked Capri on to the tarmac and Vince drove his car and trailer out of sight. 'You go ahead, Harry. I'll be along in a minute.'

'Brilliant,' chuckled Harry.

Harry arrived back in the pub just as Spike finished his game. Spike had won his singles match, despatching a grumbling, blue-shirted darter back to his team mates. 'I would have had that double sixteen normally!'

'Yeah, sure,' they sympathised.

Vince came back in and walked up to Spike.

'Well, I'll take cash!' said Spike.

'Can I have a word? But first I need a drink. George, pour me a pint, please.'

'What is it?'

'I've just had a helluva scare. You know that wall beside Ferguson's?'

'Yeah.'

'I was coming round the corner and I lost it. I'm afraid I've pranged your motor. Sorry mate!'

'What! How bad is it?'

'Eh...it's pretty bad.'

'Is it still lying up there?'

'No, it's in the car park.'

The pub had now gone quiet. Even the darts team had been distracted by this conversation. 'There's been a smash!' someone said.

Spike bounded out the door, swearing under his breath. Some of the other drinkers were up off their seats. 'Come on, Vince has pranged Spike's car!'

Vince followed Spike outside. Spike was holding his head in his hands.

'Fuck's sake! For fuck's sake!' Spike cried. 'It's fucked big time. It's a write-off. For the love of fuck, that'll never fix. Jesus Christ, for fuck's sake!'

'What happened?' asked another local who had arrived.

'I lost it at the corner at Ferguson's place. I'm OK, though.'

'For fuck's sake!' said the local.

'For fuck's sake!' said another. 'That's fucked it!'

'C'mon, Spike, I'll buy you a pint. I need one myself. I'm a bit shaken although I didn't hurt myself.'

'Christ! What happens now?' asked a dejected-looking Spike, lifting his pint in slow motion. 'My car's a write-off. I'm only third party.'

'Look, I'm sorry. I'll sort something out. Just let me have another drink. I'm still a bit shaken. George, give me a whisky, will you, and another for Spike.'

Spike had gone to have another look before it got completely dark. He came back, shaking his head and wishing he'd managed to sell it.

'Spike! You're on next. Are we playing this doubles or what?'

'My car's wrecked and you want me to play darts? For fuck's sake!'

'Mind the language, lads!' George shouted. 'There are ladies in here. Just settle down.'

'I'm sorry, mate,' said Vince. 'Let's try and be positive about this. It's only a car and you did win your singles.'

'Car...singles! Get's a whisky, George.'

'Look, you go and play your doubles. They need you on next. I'm going to the bog. We'll speak about this after,' said Vince, anxious to get on with the wind-up.

Spike stepped up in front of the board, still shaking his head. Vince nodded to Harry and they both slipped out the door. 'Bloody brilliant, Odd Job.'

'Come on. Let's get this car changed back. The best is yet to come. I can't wait to see the look on Spike's face.'

'He won't take a swing at you, will he?'

'Naw, he'll just be pissed off for a while.'

'Brilliant,' laughed Harry.

The two of them managed to push the wrecked car back on the trailer. It helped that the car was parked on a slope, making it easier to manoeuvre. Harry went round the rear and drove Spike's unmarked Capri back to the front of the pub and then drove Vince's car and trailer with the wreck on board out of sight. Vince walked in and went up to the bar.

'Are we sorting this out before we all get pissed?' asked a gloomy Spike.

'Sort what out?' George had been busy behind the bar and had just got round to asking, 'What's all this about your car, Spike?'

'It's been a shite of a day.'

'You'd better show George what's happened. After all, it's in his car park,' said Vince.

'Come on, then,' sighed Spike. 'Come and have a look at this bloody mess.'

Spike and George went out through the door along with a few others who wanted a closer look for themselves. Vince had a smirk on his face that the crowded bar had seen before.

The door burst open.

'You bastard! I'll kill you! You fuckin' bastard!'

Vince turned his head and looked at Spike and, for a moment, reflected on all the years of mischief they had been involved in since they first met. 'This one will be talked about for many years to come,' he mused.

'You shite! You had me going there for a minute.'

'A minute?'

The two of them looked at each other. 'Give us a kiss, then,' said Vince.

'Fuck you!' was the reply.

It had been a grand day.

visit my website:
www.staycheeky.com
you can download:
e-book: Stay Cheeky
e-book: Still Cheeky
e-book: Short Stories
sign up for my free blog
www.mystaycheeky.com